Ethnic Families and Children's Achievements

To Jan

*They look back to the days of childhood
as of great happiness, because those were
the days of greatest wonder, greatest
simplicity, and most vigorous imagination.*

John Ruskin

Ethnic Families and Children's Achievements

Kevin Marjoribanks
Professor of Education, University of Adelaide

Sydney
GEORGE ALLEN & UNWIN
London Boston

First published in 1980 by
George Allen & Unwin Australia Pty Ltd
8 Napier Street
North Sydney NSW 2060

National Library of Australia
Cataloguing-in-Publication entry:

Marjoribanks, Kevin.
   Ethnic families and children's achievements.

   Index.
   Bibliography.
   ISBN 0 86861 305 3

   1. Children of immigrants—Education—Australia.
   I. Title.

371′.9675′0994

Library of Congress Catalog Card Number: 79-8518

Set in 10 on 11 point Times New Roman
by Asco Trade Typesetting Ltd, Hong Kong
Printed in Hong Kong

Acknowledgments

I wish to acknowledge my appreciation for the wonderful support given to me by the children, parents and teachers who participated in the present study. Also, I want to express my particular gratitude to the University of Adelaide for supporting my work while I was a Visiting Scholar at the University of Oxford. The study was funded by the Education Research and Development Committee of Australia, and I am indebted to them for their fine assistance.

Oxford, 1979.

Contents

Tables

Figures

1

Equality of Children's Achievements: A Framework for Analysis

Perhaps the most complex problem confronting educators is how to account for inequalities in the academic achievement of children from different social status and ethnic groups. In the following chapters an empirical study is presented which investigates a significant aspect of the dilemma. An examination is made of relations between the family learning environments, attitudes to school, and academic performance of 11-year-old children from different Australian ethclass groups. Although the concept of an ethclass has not been used extensively in educational research, it represents one of the most important social categories in industrial societies. The 'boundaries' of an ethclass can be pictured if a society is imagined as being stratified horizontally into social-status groups and also divided vertically into ethnic groups. Then those sections of the social space created by the intersection of the social status and ethnic group stratifications may be designated as ethclasses. An individual's ethclass might be, for example, Southern Italian middle social status, Greek lower social status, or Anglo-Australian lower social status. Some characteristics of ethclasses are set out by Gordon (1978: 136), who suggests that

> the ethnic group is the locus of a sense of *historical identification*, while the ethclass is the locus of a sense of *participational identification*. With a person of the same social class, but of a different ethnic group, one shares behavioral similarities but not a sense of peoplehood. With those of the same ethnic group but of a different social class, one shares the sense of peoplehood but not behavioral similarities.

Although the present study focuses on the role of families, it is realised that: (a) the family is only one of the social environments affecting a child's academic achievement, and (b) educators do not agree on the appropriateness of using the family environment in explanations of inequalities in children's educational attainments. Therefore in this first chapter a conceptual framework is developed in which it is argued that the family is a necessary social environment to be included in analyses of differences in children's achievements. The argument begins by considering various definitions of equality of educational opportunity, which leads to an examination of the conflicting concepts of cultural deprivation and cultural relativism. It is then proposed that families from dominant ethclass groups have: (a) the power to decide what is 'valued' in educational systems, and (b) the means of passing onto their children cultural capital related to the achievement of the 'valued' goals of schooling. If such propositions are to be tested, then families need to be looked at within the total social context in which they operate. Therefore a general social-psychological framework for analysing inequalities in children's school outcomes is presented. From the general model a more restricted framework is selected, which is used to guide the research reported in the following chapters. During the explication of the argument an attempt is made to lay bare the assumptions and limitations of the conceptual framework.

Equality of educational opportunity

The uncertainties associated with a definition of equality of educational opportunity are expressed in discussions of the Coleman Report (1966) which investigated the availability of equal educational opportunities for children in American schools. Data for the investigation were collected from approximately 570 000 students, 60 000 teachers, and on the facilities available in some 4000 schools. When the survey was being planned, it became obvious to the researchers that no single satisfactory definition of equality of educational opportunity existed. Eventually it was decided to provide information relevant to five definitions (see Coleman, 1968, 1975). Three of the explanations emphasised inputs into schools, and they considered:

1. Differences in community inputs, such as per pupil expenditure, physical facilities and library resources.
2. Inequality defined by the degree of social and ethnic student composition of schools.
3. 'Intangible' resources such as teachers' expectations of students, teacher morale and the level of interest of the student body in learning.

It was recognised that any of these inputs might influence the impact of schools on students. But as Coleman (1968: 16) indicates, input-type definitions provide 'no suggestion of where to stop, or just how relevant these factors might be for school quality'.Because of such limitations, a fourth definition was proposed, suggesting that equality of educational opportunity is achieved when there is equality of results for children with similar social backgrounds and abilities. The fifth definition was more radical, proposing that equality is attained when the mean results of schooling for minority group children are the same as the mean results of children from the dominant group in society.

In a review of the various definitions, Coleman (1972: 149–150) suggests that the major impact of the Coleman Report was 'in *shifting* policy attention from its traditional focus on comparison of inputs . . . to a focus on output, and the effectiveness of inputs for bringing about changes in output'. Similarly, Mosteller and Moynihan (1972: 27) claim that, as a result of the Coleman research

> no study of the quality of education or the equality of educational opportunity can hope to be taken seriously unless it deals with educational achievement or other accomplishment as the principal measure of educational quality . . . educational output, not input alone, must henceforth be the central issue.

It needs to be stressed, however, that if the radical goal of attempting to achieve equality of group mean results is accepted, then there are major policy implications for educators. As Karabel and Halsey (1977) point out, adopting the radical concept of equality means eventually that a proportionate share of children from subordinated social groups must attain 'success' in numbers commensurate with their proportions in the population. One possible consequence is that schools need to become actively involved in designing programmes aimed at reducing the differences in mean academic outcomes of children from identifiable social groups. Such programmes are likely to require policies of positive discrimination involving a redistribution of educational resources. In what is labelled the 'principle of redress', Rawls (1971: 100–101) sets forth an argument supporting policies of positive discrimination. He proposes that

> undeserved inequalities call for redress; and since inequalities of birth and natural endowment are undeserved, these inequalities are somehow to be compensated for. Thus the principle holds that in order to treat all persons equally, to provide genuine equality of opportunity, society must give more attention to those with fewer native assets and to those born into the less favorable social positions. The idea is to redress the bias of contingencies in the direction of equality. In pursuit of this principle greater resources

might be spent on the education of the less rather than the more intelligent, at least over a certain time of life, say the earlier years of school.

Although many educators now adopt output-type definitions of equality of educational opportunity, by no means has there been a universal acceptance of the more radical interpretation. One aspect of the reluctance to embrace such an interpretation of equality is summed up by Entwistle (1977: 16). He claims that

> The conclusion has to be that since both individual and group inequalities are unacceptable, we are really faced with decisions about the priority involved in removing two injustices, and cannot take refuge behind the assumption that the principle of equality is satisfied when inequalities between groups are diminished.

Entwistle goes onto suggest that

> Attacking group inequalities first may be politically expedient where persisting social inequality seems a greater threat to social order than do the inequalities suffered by marginal individuals and families within any social group. But the decision to opt for eliminating the more visible, potentially explosive inequalities between groups seems acceptable only in the language of priorities.

The conflict between espousing either a liberal explanation of equality of access or an explanation based on equality of group outcomes is reflected also in the work of Porter (1975) and Bell (1977). While agreeing that positive discrimination policies may be necessary when it is clear that discrimination and deprivation bear heavily on minority groups, Porter (1975: 297) cautions that 'The organization of society on the basis of rights or claims that derive from group membership is sharply opposed to the concept of a society based on citizenship.' And Bell (1977: 612) indicates that

> The liberal and radical attack on discrimination was *based on its denial of a justly earned place to a person on the basis of an unjust group attribute.* That person was not judged as an individual, but was judged—and excluded—because he was a member of a particular group. But now it is being demanded that one must have a place primarily because one possesses a particular group attribute. The person himself has disappeared. Only attributes remain.

Bell then proposes that, according to the radical critique of contemporary society

> an individual is treated not as a person but as a multiple of roles

that divide and fragment him and reduce him to a single dominant attribute of the major role or function he or she plays in society. ... we now find that a person is to be given preference by virtue of a role, his group membership.

In the research presented in the following chapters, differences in both group mean achievement scores and individual scores for children within ethclasses are examined. It is an assumption of the study that in the short-term the most pressing educational-political problem is to reduce gaps in the mean achievement levels of children from different ethclasses. Previous research findings have shown that when such achievement gaps exist for children in elementary schools, they become increasingly exaggerated by the time children reach secondary schools. While these latter results support policies of positive discrimination for young children from different subordinated social groups, the present study assumes that policies must also be directed at diminishing the wide discrepancies that occur in the educational attainments of children from within the same ethclass groups (see Jencks, 1972).

If educational policies are designed to reduce group differences in children's achievements, then conclusions from much previous research emphasise the necessity of incorporating in such policies considerations of family learning environments. Coleman (1975: 27), for example, proposes that 'perhaps the most pervasive research result of recent research in educational achievement, ..., is the strength of the effect of family differences in creating achievement differences among children, compared to the relative weakness of effect of school differences.' From a re-analysis of the Coleman Report data, Armor (1972: 225) asserts that if differentials in achievement among children from different social groups are to be reduced, then programmes 'should give as much attention, if not more, to the environment—both family and neighborhood—in which the minority child lives.' Similarly, Smith (1972) concludes that schools have little influence on achievement which is independent of the child's background and general social context. Commenting on the educational expansion in industrial societies during the 1950s and 1960s, Halsey (1972: 8) suggests that 'in terms of relative chances of income, status and welfare at birth, the impact of the educational system on the life of children remained heavily determined by their family and class origins.' He makes the strong assertion that liberal policies of equality failed because they were related to an inadequate theory of learning. 'They failed to notice that the major determinants of educational attainment were not schoolmasters but social institutions, not curriculum but motivation, not formal access to school but support in the family and in the community.' And Midwinter (1975: 61) insists that, 'No matter how much you do *inside* the school, you can make virtually no impact at all without the informed support of the home.' He claims that the family, peer group, and neighbourhood 'whether we like it or not, are the true and influential educators; we ignore them at our peril.'

From such conclusions, emphasising the importance of relations between families and children's achievements, educational programmes have been developed which may be categorised as reflecting a 'cultural deprivation' interpretation of inequalities. Such an interpretation has met with trenchant opposition and has been replaced by many educators with a 'cultural relativism' explanation of children's differences in school achievement. In the following section of the chapter it is suggested that programmes developed to reduce inequalities in children's academic achievement need to be based on a model incorporating elements of both explanations.

Cultural deprivation and cultural relativism

The concept of cultural deprivation maintains that children from certain minority ethclasses enter schools deficient in academic skills and that the deficiencies are associated with inadequacies in the family learning environments of the children. Therefore educational programmes attempt to 'compensate' for the alleged 'deficiencies' of minority group families. Opponents of such an explanation state that minority group children and their families do not have deficient cultures. Instead, it is argued that such cultures are merely different from mainstream culture, but they are made to appear deficient because they have imposed upon them those definitions of reality of the mainstream group. From such opposition an interpretation of inequality has been generated directing attention from the alleged deficiencies of children and their families to the failings of schools. According to this cultural difference position or cultural relativism interpretation, once teachers accept minority group cultures as being valid on their own terms, then many of the problems confronting teachers and children are likely to disappear. As Bernstein (1970: 347) suggests

> We need to distinguish between the principles and operations that teachers transmit and develop in the children, and the contexts

they create in order to do this. We should start knowing that the social experience the child already possesses is valid and significant, and that this social experience should be reflected back to him as being valid and significant.

And he proposes that children's social experiences can only be reflected back to them if it is part of the texture of the learning experiences created by teachers.

The cultural relativism approach has been extremely valuable in redressing many of the excesses of extreme social pathology or cultural deficit positions. But there are difficulties associated with the application of the approach. A major decision has to be made whether to change the goals of education for children from different social groups or whether different means of achieving similar goals should be adopted. In an attack on cultural deficit models, Baratz and Baratz (1970: 41), for example, claim that 'the failure lies in the schools, not the parents, to educate these children ... critical intervention must be done, but on the procedures and materials used in the schools rather than on the children those schools service.' They suggest that new classroom procedures and materials that are culturally relevant for children from different ethclasses are critically needed. But while encouraging the adoption of new teaching methods and a more appropriate curriculum, the Baratz emphasise that it is the process and not the goals of schooling which must be changed for minority group children. In a critique of the Baratz position, Edwards and Hargreaves (1976) observe that by: (a) emphasising means rather than ends, and (b) having as one of its aims the removal of minority group children's 'handicaps' so they can negotiate with mainstream culture, the approach does not differ significantly from the deficit position. A more forceful attack of the Baratz position is offered by Keddie (1972: 131). She argues that the Baratz cultural diversity model is restricted, 'not to say a sham, since the validity of black culture is limited to its use in helping a child to become "acculturated" to the "real" culture of the "mainstream".' But an extension of Keddie's (1973: 16) argument, suggesting that 'the insistence on literacy is peculiar to school education and not to the life-worlds of learners', is itself condemned for not taking adequate cognizance of the realities of societal power (e.g. see Glennerster and Hatch, 1974; Harris, 1974; Robinson, 1976; Entwistle, 1977; Giles and Woolfe, 1977).

The approach adopted in the present research assumes that families as well as schools are significant social contexts influencing children's achievements. In an attempt to accommodate the strengths of both the cultural deprivation and cultural relativism positions, within one explanation of children's inequalities, a theory of cultural transmission is explored in the following section of the chapter. Essentially, the theoretical position claims that middle social-status families have: (a) the power to decide what type of school achievement will be rewarded by society, and (b) in relation to minority social groups they have greater means of creating learning environments associated with children's 'successful' achievement.

Family transmission of cultural capital

A sociological framework for studying relations between social groups and the transmission of cultural capital has been provided by Weber. He proposes that the ideal of the cultivated person adopted in a given society is the outcome of the power of the dominant social group to universalise its particular cultural ideal (also see, Karabel and Halsey, 1977; Persell, 1977). Weber (1948: 426) claims that

> The pedagogy of cultivation, finally, attempts to *educate* a cultivated type of man, whose nature depends on the decisive stratum's respective ideal of cultivation. And this means to educate a man for a certain internal and external deportment in life. In principle this can be done with everybody, only the goal differs.

From analyses of ancient cultures Weber concludes, for example, that 'If a separate stratum of warriors form the decisive status group ... education will aim at making the pupil a stylised knight and courtier.... If a priestly stratum is decisive, it will aim at making the disciple a scribe, or at least an intellectual.' From an investigation of the Chinese Literati, Weber (1948: 427) indicates that, 'The Chinese examinations did not test any special skills, as do our modern rational and bureaucratic examination regulations for jurists, medical doctors, or technicians.' Instead, the examinations 'tested whether or not the candidate's mind was thoroughly steeped in literature and whether or not he possessed the *ways of thought* suitable to a cultured man and resulting from cultivation in literature' (1948: 428). These extracts from Weber suggest that if certain social groups have the power to determine what is valued in the educational system at a particular time in history, then it is not surprising to find that subordinated social groups are disadvantaged in relation to the criteria set by the dominant social groups.

For the present research it is assumed that: (a) in industrial societies, children with highly developed 'standard' linguistic abilities and numerical skills generally are rewarded favourably, and (b) in relation to subordinated social groups, the dominant social group possesses greater means of creating for their children family learning environments that are more strongly related to the acquisition of the valued achievement skills. The significant role of families in providing children with the means of acquiring the code necessary to interpret the message of the dominant culture is expressed by Bourdieu (1973: 80–81), when he states that

> an institution officially entrusted with the transmission of the instruments of appropriation of the dominant culture which neglects methodically to transmit the instruments indispensable to the success of its undertaking is bound to become the monopoly of those social classes capable of transmitting by their own means, that is to say by that diffuse and implicit continuous educational action which operates within cultured families (often unknown to those responsible for it and to those who are subjected to it), the instruments necessary for the reception of its message, and thereby to confirm their monopoly of the instruments of appropriation of the dominant culture and thus their monopoly of that culture.

In the following research the social-psychological learning environment created by parents is considered a significant element of the cultural capital transmitted from families to children. Also, it is assumed that children who eventually are rewarded by society for their academic success are likely, in relation to other children, to achieve higher levels of numeracy and 'standard' literacy by the end of elementary school. For the analysis of family learning environments the ideal-typical theory used by Weber to define sociological concepts is adopted, and in Chapter 2 an 'academically oriented family-type' is constructed from the findings of previous research. Learning environments of families from different ethclasses are then analysed in relation to the ideal family-type and also related to children's attitudes to school and to their academic achievement.

Thus, the conceptual framework being developed for the research proposes that in analyses of inequalities in children's educational attainments, it is necessary to analyse differences between the learning environments of families from mainstream culture and those from social groups in minority power situations. It is hoped that the findings of such research will assist educators in constructing new learning contexts for minority group children. It is proposed that these learning contexts should involve interactions between classroom, neighbourhood and family environments, and they should assist children in acquiring those skills that are necessary in order to negotiate with mainstream social groups. The previous statement should not be interpreted as meaning that the environments of families from ethclasses in minority power positions are deficient. What the framework is attempting to highlight is that because of the realities of the distribution of power within society, certain ethclasses are disadvantaged in relation to the creation of learning environments associated with those achievements rewarded in society. As Giles and Woolfe (1977: 58) state, 'the reality of the situation is that certain kinds of behaviour, speech and ways of acting give access to power, income and resources to some groups and, conversely, deny them to others.' They propose that while members from a minority culture may possess a coherent and complex cultural linguistic system, unless they learn to perform adequately in the wider social context their options will be considerably reduced. Thus, educators need to be extremely cautious when constructing educational programmes, for certain groups of children, that do not recognise the existing realities of the distribution of power in a society and which may limit the educational and occupational options of those children. It is a premise of the present research that while children develop as full members of their own ethclass, they should be encouraged to acquire skills permitting them to negotiate with and operate in more powerful social groups. I am very sensitive to the potential conflicts that occur in the allegiances of children who grow up in 'two social worlds'. But I have sympathy for the position of Giles and Woolfe (1977: 59), that 'we do not help the poor and "deprived" by denying them access to basic learning skills on the grounds that this represents cultural colonisation.' If members of subordinated ethclasses are to challenge successfully existing patterns of societal power, then I suggest that they will be in a stronger position to do so if they acquire the academic skills valued by the more powerful social groups. As Gramsci (1971: 40) suggests, in his analysis of the Italian educational system, the social character of schools

> is determined by the fact that each social group has its own type of school, intended to perpetuate a specific traditional function, ruling or subordinate. If one wishes to break this pattern one needs, instead of multiplying and grading different types of vocational school, to create a single type of formative school (primary-secondary) which would take the child up to the threshold of his choice of job, forming him during this time as a person capable of thinking, studying, and ruling-or controlling those who rule.... Political democracy tends towards a coincidence of the rulers and the ruled ... ensuring for each nonruler a

free training in the skills and general technical preparation necessary to that end.

As stated earlier, the family is only one learning environment associated with a child's academic achievement. In the following section of the chapter a more complete model for examining inequalities in children's academic achievement is presented.

General conceptual framework for the analysis of inequalities in children's academic achievement

A general social-psychological framework for examining differences in children's achievements would incorporate analyses of classroom and school contexts, peer group and neighbourbood influences, family learning environments, the individual characteristics of children, and children's interpretations of their environmental situations. The model presented in Figure 1.1 is an attempt to locate the family experience within the social context in which it operates. In the model it is suggested that academic achievement is related to: children's interpretations of social situations, their own personality characteristics such as self concept, attitudes to school, intellectual abilities and locus of control, and also to the social-psychological structural aspects of environments. The interrelations between structural and interpretative influences on behaviour have been set out by Berger and Luckmann (1971: 151). They suggest that

> Every individual is born into an objective social structure within which he encounters the significant others who are in charge of his socialization. These significant others are imposed upon him.... The significant others who mediate this world to him modify it in the course of mediating it. They select aspects of it in accordance with their own location in the social structure, and also by virtue of their individual, biographically rooted idiosyncrasies. The social world is 'filtered' to the individual through this double selectivity. Thus the lower-class child not only absorbs a lower-class per spective on the social world, he absorbs it in the idiosyncratic coloration given it by his parents (or whatever other individuals are in charge of his primary socialization).

While the framework is necessarily static in its presentation, it is meant to reflect a set of dynamic processes in which all the elements of the model operate within an interactive system. An attempt has

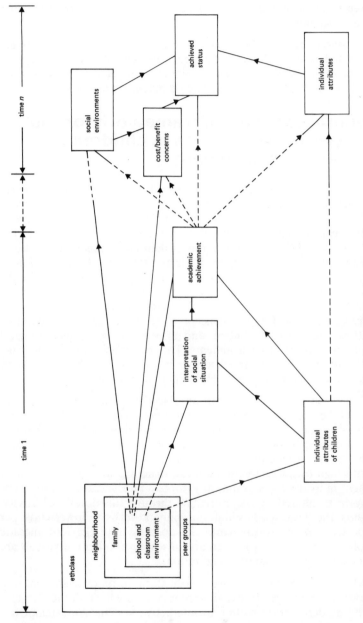

Figure 1.1 General Framework for Analysis of Educational Attainment

been made to portray the dynamic nature of the relationships by presenting the model as a longitudinal set of processes. Those relationships depicted as operating at time 1 are assumed to influence a similar set of relations at successive time periods, until time n. The final variable in the framework, which is labelled achieved status, represents interrelationships between measures of: amount of education attained, the occupation achieved, and income earned. Such a combination of achieved status variables has been used in recent sociological path analytic studies of the relations between children's social-status background and measures of their educational and occupational attainment (e.g. see Sewell and Hauser, 1972; Haller and Portes, 1973; Alexander *et al.*, 1975; Wilson and Portes, 1975; Hauser *et al.*, 1976; Picou and Carter, 1976; Portes, 1976; Portes and Wilson, 1976; Alwin and Otto, 1977; and De Bord *et al.* 1977). Towards the end of the model a cost-benefit measure has been included. Boudon (1974: 21) proposes that 'the social status individuals achieve is the result of a two-stage filtering process. In the first stage they go from a given social background to a given educational level. In the second stage they go from educational level to achieved status.' But he suggests that, 'reaching a given educational level or a given status means being exposed to costs and benefits that are going to differ according to social background' (1974: 23). It is hoped that the total model indicates the complexity of understanding inequalities in children's school outcomes. In the present research a more modest framework is used to guide the investigation and it is presented in the following section of the chapter.

Research framework adopted for present investigation

The model shown in Figure 1.2 has been adopted in the present investigation. It concentrates on relations between academic achievement, individual characteristics of children, and the social-psychological learning environments of families (as defined by parents) from different ethclasses. It is realised that in more comprehensive analyses, the arrows depicting relationships among the variables would, in most cases, involve two-way processes. While not investigating statistical reciprocal actions, the model is meant to reflect an interactionism framework of analysis. In social-psychological and educational empirical research, children's behaviour has typically been examined in relation to one of the

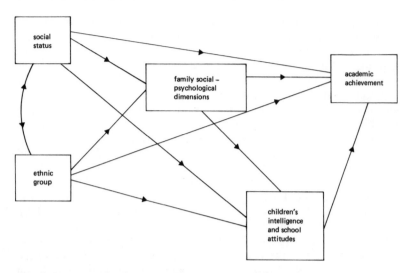

Figure 1.2 Conceptual model for present analysis

following three models: (a) the trait model, (b) the situationism model, and (c) the interactionism framework. In the trait model, factors determining behaviour are considered to be within the persons themselves. As Endler and Magnusson (1976: 6) suggest, in the 'classical' trait theory

> it is sufficient to merely study the individual. Situations are taken into account, but the provoking and restricting effect of situational factors on behaviour is not supposed to change the rank order of individuals for a given trait. This means that the rank order of individuals for any given trait is supposed to be the same for different situations independent of the situational characteristics, except for errors of measurement.

In contrast, the situationism position regards situational factors or the stimuli in the situation, as the main determinants of individual behaviour. It is an assumption of this present research that behaviour is the result of an indispensable, continuous interaction between persons and the situations they encounter. That is, differences in children's school achievement are explained most appropriately by examining an interactionism framework of behaviour. In this latter model it is assumed that not only do situations influence individuals, but that individuals select and subsequently influence the situations with which they interact (see Marjoribanks, 1979a). Argyle (1976:

173) offers a warning, however, that 'We should not exaggerate the power individuals have to change situations; some people have very little effect and some situations can't be changed much.' Similarly, Karabel and Halsey (1977: 58) propose that

> Stress on the fact that relations in educational institutions are humanly constructed products is a welcome antidote to the deterministic and reifying tendencies of some of the 'old' sociology of education. But emphasis on 'man the creator' often fails to take adequate account of the social constraints on human actors in everyday life.

They suggest that there is 'a considerable latitude available to those engaged in struggles over the "definition of the situation", but the question of whose definition will ultimately prevail is preeminently one of *power*.' The following study considers that family learning environments are the result of interactive processes such that their properties are determined by the characteristics of parents, the influence of other social contexts, and the influence of children's behaviours and achievements on the attitudes and aspirations of parents.

One of the earliest social-psychological forms of the interactionism framework was developed by Lewin (1935) in his field theory of personality. Part of his framework is adapted for the present study, with the elements of the model being presented in Figure 1.3 (see Deutsch, 1968; Hall and Lindzey, 1970). Stated simply, the model shows that the person (P) is surrounded by the social-psychological environment of the family (E), while the behaviour (B) of the person

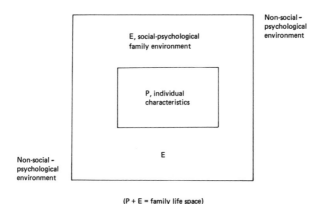

(P + E = family life space)

Figure 1.3 Adaptation from Lewin's field theory of personality

is a function of both the person characteristics and the environment. That is, $B = f(P,E)$. The social-psychological family environment is considered to be surrounded by other environmental influences such as social status and ethnicity, with the boundary between the family life space and the 'outer world' being endowed with the property of permeability. As Hall and Lindzey (1970: 215) suggest, 'The implication of a permeable boundary between the life space and the physical world is of far-reaching significance. A fact in the non social-psychological world of the family may radically change the whole course of events in the life space, so that prediction from a knowledge of social-psychological data alone is usually limited.' Lewin also indicates that the boundary between the person and the environment is permeable, such that the environment can influence the person, $P = f(E)$, and person variables can influence the environment, $E = f(P)$.

A restricted model of the interactionism framework is adopted in some of the later analyses, when the academic achievement of children is related to the interaction between measures of the social-psychological environment of the family and the person variables of children's intelligence and their cognitive and affective attitudes towards schooling. It is restricted in the sense that ideally an interactionism framework would incorporate a dynamic or organismic, rather than a reactive or mechanistic, model of the individual (see Harré and Secord, 1972). In mechanistic models, interactions are between causes rather than between chains of causes and effects. That is, the mechanistic framework (see Figure 1.2) is concerned with unidirectional relations and assumes that independent variables are associated with dependent measures. Endler and Magnusson (1976: 13) state that the dynamic model is concerned with a reciprocal action 'so that not only do events affect the behaviour of organisms, but the organism is also an active agent in influencing environmental events'. But they go on to say that in the social sciences, we have not yet developed fully the methodology and technology necessary to investigate the nature of dynamic interaction.

A criticism of the person environment schema is offered by de Waele and Harré (1976: 196), who suggest that the approach is not yet sufficiently sophisticated. They propose that

> Neither situation nor person can be generalised, and at the heart of this perception is the realisation that a person, conceived as the bearer of certain social competences, has a unique structure, intelligible only because it contains many universal elements, coordinated in their social meaning by a social language. But 'situation'

is not an independent 'variable' in this 'function'. Situations are constructed and endowed with meaning by people in terms of those very same cognitive resources upon which their social competence depends, and are only mildly constrained by their person-independent parameters.

While the ethogenic interpretation of social action provides many potentially exciting challenges for educational research (e.g. see Harré, 1976; Marsh *et al.* 1978), de Waele and Harré (1976: 198) indicate the present difficulties of pursuing such research. They note that 'In recent years there have been many attempts to apply concepts originally developed in ethology to the analysis of human social life. We do not believe that these attempts have yet risen much above the level of journalism.'

The research presented in the following chapters is within the framework of a structural analysis of family environments. But it is recognised that detailed and sensitive studies need to be undertaken which adopt an indicative-eliminative-type methodology and examine relations between: the academic performance of children from different ethclasses, the biographies of children, and the 'cognitive and perceived and interpreted environmental conditions which shape the spontaneous flow of a person's actions into a meaningful structure' (de Waele and Harré, 1976: 192). The findings of such research will provide data to embellish studies such as the present one, which observe the social-psychological structure of families.

Thus, although it is assumed throughout the research that situations are a function of the person, and person's behaviour is a function of the situation, the research supports Endler's (1976: 66) contention that 'Concurrent with an investigation of dynamic interaction we must also examine how persons and situations interact (mechanistic interaction) in influencing behaviour.'

In the following chapter the methodology of the research is presented and an ideal-typical definition of an 'academically oriented family' is constructed. Chapters 3 and 4 examine ethclass differences in measures of family environment, children's person characteristics, and children's academic achievement. In Chapter 5 interrelationships between the behaviour, person and environment variables for children within different ethclasses are investigated, using regression surface analyses. The final chapter explores some potential policy implications of the research. As stated earlier, although the research concentrates on family environments, it is realised that other social contexts have highly significant associations with children's achievement. It is hoped that the present investigation encourages detailed examinations of other environmental correlates of the school outcomes of children from Australian ethclass groups, and that these investigations adopt a variety of conceptual frameworks and methodologies to assess the environmental situations.

2

Academically Oriented Families: Design of the Study

As indicated in Chapter 1, the present study analyses relationships between family environments and the school-related attitudes and cognitive performance of children from different Australian ethclasses. In this chapter, the design of the research is presented, including an explanation of the sample, the construction of an ideal-typical definition of an academically oriented family, and a description of the measures used to assess family learning environments, children's school attitudes and their cognitive performance.

Sample

The data for the study were collected from families belonging to six Australian ethclasses, comprising 140 Anglo-Australian middle social-status families, and lower social-status families from the following groups: Anglo-Australian (250 families), English (120), Greek (170), Southern Italian (120) and Yugoslavian (50). Family social status was based on an equally weighted composite of father's occupation and the education of the mother and father. For fatherless families, if the mother was employed her occupation was used in constructing the composite. Each family had a child, approximately 11 years old, attending either a Roman Catholic or government-supported urban elementary school. In each ethclass, the samples include nearly equal numbers of girls and boys. Findings from the research need to be interpreted within the limitation that the total sample is a purposive one, and not random. Attempts are made throughout the analysis, however, to make adjustments for the design effects of the sample by recalculating significance levels, using the formula: standard error of sample estimate $= $ (design effect)$^{\frac{1}{2}} \times$ simple random standard error (see Kish, 1965; Ross, 1976).

The particular immigrant groups were selected for the study as they represent, numerically, four of the largest ethnic groups in

Australia. A family was designated as belonging to an ethclass only if both parents were members of that ethclass. In Anglo-Australian families, both parents were born in Australia and English was the only language spoken in the home. For the Greek, Southern Italian and Yugoslavian families, the median period of residence in Australia for both parents was approximately sixteen years, while for English parents it was ten years. The English sample was restricted to families from England. Although only a relatively small number of Yugoslavian families were sampled, they were retained in the analysis as they revealed, in relation to other non-Anglo families, a different pattern of English use. For example, 89 and 85 per cent of Greek mothers and fathers, respectively, stated they spoke Greek 'all' or 'most of the time' in the home. These percentages increase to 96 and 94, when a category is included indicating that Greek is used at least 'half of the time'. In Southern Italian homes, the corresponding percentages associated with speaking Italian 'all' or 'most of the time' are 76 and 72 for mothers and fathers, and 92 and 85 when the category 'half of the time' is included. For Yugoslavian mothers and fathers, however, 56 and 54 per cent, respectively, stated they used English 'all' or 'most of the time' in the home. Thus, while the Yugoslavian sample size is small, the group appears to represent an intermediate position in the use of English, between the Anglo-ethclasses and the Greek and Southern Italian groups. And, as Thomas and Znaniecki (1958) suggest, relations between social organisation and individual life organisation are most suitably examined by a comparative analysis of social groups in different positions of transition from older to newer organisational forms.

Generally, 3 per cent of families in each ethclass had only one parent, while in the Anglo-Australian lower social-status group the number approached 8 per cent. These families were not selected for special analysis, as their actual numbers within each ethclass are relatively small. Also, data were not collected on how long these families had had only one parent, nor on the reasons for the absence of the second parent. It is recognised, however, that future studies will need to analyse one-parent families as a special category. Some of the other social-structural characteristics of the families are shown in Table 2.1. The figures indicate, for example, that a large proportion of mothers were employed. Typically, they were involved in occupations classified within the lowest levels of the social-status structure. Except for the Yugoslavians, only about 10 per cent of families had 'other' adults living with them. Generally, it was only one 'other' adult, suggesting that within the home, family structures approached more closely a nuclear rather than an extended pattern.

TABLE 2.1 *Social characteristics of ethclass families*

SOCIAL CHARACTERISTICS	ETHCLASS					
	A	B	C	D	E	F
Percentage of families with:						
Working mothers	59	52	48	60	35	49
One or more other adults living with them	10	8	23	12	13	9
Three or more children	54	79	63	69	76	67
Five or more children	2	20	23	21	25	19
Average number of children per family	2.7	3.6	4.0	3.6	3.8	3.6
Mother's education	1.9	1.8	2.1	2.9	2.8	3.8
Father's education	2.0	1.9	2.3	2.8	2.8	4.0
Average social-status index (ANU 2 Scale)	382	398	388	439	420	582

A = Greek   D = English
B = Southern Italian   E = Anglo-Australian lower status
C = Yugoslavian   F = Anglo-Australian middle status

These findings do not, of course, take into account associations between related families within a neighbourhood. Except for Greek families, the sibsize figures show that average family sizes in each ethclass are quite similar. The variation for Greek families may possibly be explained by differences in the sibling structures of families. Approximately 77 per cent of the Greek 11-year-olds are either first- or second-born children, while in the other ethclasses the corresponding figure approaches 55 per cent. These data suggest that the average-age structure of Greek siblings may be younger than those in the other groups and that at the time of the study there may have been fewer completed Greek families.

The parents' education data represent averages of ratings from question 21 in Part B of the family environment schedule, constructed for the study (see Appendix A). A rating of 2, 3 or 4 indicates parents completed elementary school, finished some secondary school, or completed secondary school, respectively. Typically, the averaged ratings show that non-Anglo parents completed elementary school, the lower social-status Anglo-Australian and English groups had some secondary school education, while parents in the Anglo-Australian middle social-status group completed secondary school. The final row of figures in Table 2.1 gives social-status ratings, based on the ANU 2 Scale. The Scale, which ranks over 400 occupations within the Australian social context, was constructed at the Australian National University and has a range of ratings from 331 to 915. In relation to the averaged ratings, the three non-Anglo groups are in the intermediate levels of the lower social-status structure, while the Anglo-Australian and English groups are in the intermediate to upper levels of that status structure. For the Anglo-Australian middle social-status families, the averaged ratings place families in the lower to intermediate levels of the middle social-status hierarchy. Although the distributions of lower social-status families across the ethnic groups are quite comparable, the use of an elongated social-status index shows the often unacknowledged difficulty of 'equating' such distributions. These social-status variations across ethnic groups are taken into account in some of the later analyses. The sample therefore consists of 850 families drawn from six Australian ethclasses.

Academically oriented families: an ideal type

An ideal-typical definition of an academically oriented family is constructed in the following section of the chapter. In Chapter 1 it was proposed that such families, because of their situation in the power structure of society, create social-psychological learning environments that are closely related to their children's successful school academic achievement. The ideal-type definition is used as a framework for constructing a family environment schedule that is adopted in the remainder of the analysis.

Before an academically oriented family is defined, it is important to stress that an ideal type is not related to an ideal in any ethical sense. Instead, it is a model of a phenomenon that extracts the essential or 'pure' elements of the phenomenon. The concept of 'ideal' refers to the abstract nature of the 'type', not to its desirability. As Freund (1968: 62–64) suggests, 'the ideal type is not intended to be in any way exemplary, and must not be confused with an ethical model, or even with a practical rule of conduct. It seeks perfection of a logical, not a moral, order, and it excludes all value judgments.' She also indicates that

> Such a conceptual construct is 'ideal' in that it is never, or only very rarely, encountered in all its purity in real life. ... because it is unreal and takes us a step away from reality, it enables us to obtain a better intellectual and scientific grasp of reality, although necessarily a fragmented one.

Weber proposed that an ideal type is formed by

> the one-sided accentuation of one or more points of view and by
> the synthesis of a great many diffuse, discrete, more or less present
> and occasionally absent concrete individual phenomena, which are
> arranged according to those one-sidedly emphasized viewpoints
> into a unified analytical construct. (see Shils and Finch, 1949: 90.)

For the present research, the ideal type of an academically oriented
family is constructed from the findings of studies that have examined
the 'alpha' press of families. The concept of an environmental press
comes from Murray's (1938) theory of personality, which proposes
that environments surrounding individuals may be thought of as
consisting of press variables having the potential for either harming
or benefiting different individuals, or of influencing the same individual in different ways at different times. Murray suggests that an
individual's own interpretation of the perceived environment might
be labelled the environment's beta press, while 'the press that actually
exists, as far as scientific discovery can determine it', is designated as
the environment's alpha press (1938: 122).

The beta press and family environments

The most detailed and exhaustive analysis of the beta press of social
environments has been undertaken by Professor Moos and his as-
sociates at the Social Ecology Laboratory in the Stanford University
School of Medicine. They have developed perceived social climate
scales to measure environments such as: psychiatric wards,
community-oriented psychiatric treatment programmes, correctional
institutions, military basic training companies, university student
residences, junior and high school classrooms, work situations, thera-
peutic and decision-making groups, and families (e.g. see Moos, 1974,
1975, 1979; Trickett and Moos, 1973). Common social-psychological
dimensions have emerged from investigations of each of these different kinds of social environments, and they have been concep-
tualised by Moos (e.g. Moos, 1973, 1979; Hearn and Moos, 1978) in
three broad categories: relationship dimensions, personal development or goal orientation dimensions, and system maintenance and
change dimensions. As Insel and Moos (1974: 181) state, these broad
categories are similar across the different environments 'although
vastly different settings may impose unique variations within the
general categories'. Typically, relationship dimensions assess the
extent to which individuals are involved in the environment and how
much they help and support each other, while the personal develop-

ment dimensions consider the opportunity or potential in the environment for personal growth and the development of self-esteem. The system maintenance and system change dimensions measure whether environments are orderly and clear in their expectations, how they maintain control, and if they are responsive to change. A Family Environment Scale has been developed (see Moos and Moos, 1976) to describe family social environments as perceived by the family members themselves. The scale consists of ninety true-false items, loading on ten subscales, each measuring the emphasis of one dimension of family environment. Relationship dimensions are assessed by scales labelled cohesion, expressiveness and conflict, while the personal-growth dimensions are measured by scales called independence, achievement orientation, intellectual-cultural orientation, active-recreational and a moral-religious emphasis. Two scales for the system-maintenance dimension are labelled organisation and control. The Moos framework has been described in some detail as it represents one of the most elegant attempts to understand individuals' interpretations of their perceptions of social environments. From an investigation of responses to the family environment questionnaire, Moos and Moos (1976) have constructed a typology of family social environments. In the typology there are six distinct family types: expression-oriented, structure-oriented, independence-oriented, achievement-oriented, moral/religious-oriented and conflict-oriented. For the present study, the most relevant type includes the achievement-oriented families which are characterised by 'a strong emphasis on placing different types of activities (i.e., school and work) into an achievement-oriented or competitive framework. These families are particularly interested in working hard and getting ahead in life' (Moos and Moos, 1976: 362). Two clusters of achievement-oriented families were observed, those stressing achievement orientation in a framework of independence, and those emphasising achievement in a context of conformity. Achievement-independence families pursue activities in a competitive manner, while encouraging their members to be assertive, self-sufficient, to make their own decisions and to think things out for themselves. Achievement-conforming families stress conformity, 'as indicated by their extremely low scores on Independence' (Moos and Moos, 1976: 364). It is suggested that, 'The major difference between the two types of Achievement-Oriented families is that independence is emphasized in one type and de-emphasized in the other' (1976: 364).

An extremely fruitful perspective from which to analyse the beta press of family social environments is provided by Moos' conceptual framework and methodology. The results of his research into families suggest that press for achievement orientation and press for independence might be two dimensions for possible inclusion in a definition of an academically oriented family. Research generated from the Moos family schedule, however, has not yet produced data on relations between the beta press measures and children's academic achievement. Instead, the most detailed studies relating children's achievements and their perceptions of family environments have used extremely restricted family measures. These investigations form part of an expanding sociological research literature using path analytic techniques to trace relations between sets of social-background measures, children's early cognitive scores, significant others' influences, children's expectations and assessments of eventual social-status attainment. Typically, these studies show that students' perceptions of parental encouragement are associated quite strongly with later educational attainments. While the analyses, although not without criticism, are becoming increasingly sophisticated in their application of statistical techniques, the assessment of variables is often extremely restricted. For example, the parent index is generally assessed by one item, requiring students to respond to a question such as: how much encouragement have you received from your parents to attend college? Path analytic studies of children's educational attainments will only have meaningful educational implications when they include more sensitive social-environmental measures. Thus, as existing research of the beta press of family environments for elementary school-age children provides few findings that are applicable for the construction of our ideal type, the present research relies on findings generated from studies of the alpha press of family environments.

The alpha press and family environments

As already indicated, Murray defined the alpha press of an environment as 'the press that actually exists, as far as scientific discovery can determine it' (1938: 122). Bloom (1964) offers a similar definition when suggesting that environments may be thought of as the conditions, forces and external stimuli impinging on individuals. He proposes that these forces, which may be physical, social as well as intellectual, provide a network surrounding, engulfing and playing on the individual. It is acknowledged that some individuals may resist the network, but it is considered likely that few individuals will be able to avoid completely the environmental forces. The latter proposition is in sympathy, for example, with Argyle's (1976) caveat, cited in Chapter 1, that the power individuals have to change their situations should not be exaggerated, but is opposed by researchers adopting interpretative frameworks emphasising the significance of understanding the meaning attached to social behaviour by the individuals themselves. The present study does not agree with a 'strong' interpretation of the Bloom position that it is only the extreme and rare individuals who can avoid or escape from family environmental forces. Instead, it is assumed that family environments, as defined by parents, establish sets of constraints which are, in part, influenced by children's individual characteristics but which also interact with children's characteristics in affecting achievement.

A number of studies, generated from Bloom's framework, have identified a set of social-psychological family environment variables that have moderate to high concurrent validities in relation to academic achievement and low to moderate associations with intelligence (e.g. Dave, 1963; Wolf, 1964; Dyer, 1967; Mosychuk, 1969; Keeves, 1972; Levine *et al.*, 1972; Marjoribanks, 1972*a*, 1974*a*; Kellaghan, 1977; and Trotman, 1977, 1978). Most of these investigations have been examined in detail elsewhere (see Marjoribanks, 1979*b*) and therefore they are not analysed here. From the studies, four environment dimensions that have strong associations with children's achievement can be extracted to form the framework for the definition of an academically oriented family. These dimensions are: (a) parents' achievement orientations, which are related to processes such as whether parents ever discuss their child's progress, how often parents praise their children for doing well at school, how much time parents expect their children to devote to homework, and how familiar parents are with their children's activities at school, (b) family press for English, which considers parents' concern for, and use of, English within the home, and also family reading habits, (c) press for independence, which gauges whether parents indicate to their children that they expect them to be self-reliant while at the same time granting them relative autonomy in decision-making situations, and (d) educational-occupational aspirations, which express how much education and what type of occupation parents would like their children to achieve. Also, these dimensions, or variations of them, have strong associations with measures of academic achievement in another set of studies, using data on British children (e.g. Fraser, 1959; Peaker, 1967, 1971; Plowden Report, 1967; Wiseman, 1967; Bynner, 1972; Marjoribanks, 1976*a*).

Three of the selected dimensions, achievement orientations, press for independence, and aspirations, are similar to components of the achievement syndrome developed by Rosen (1956, 1959, 1961). He proposes that family learning environments may be characterised by variations in the interrelated components of: achievement training, independence training, achievement-value orientations, and educational-vocational aspirations. It is suggested that achievement training and independence training act together to generate achievement motivation, which provides children with the internal psychological impetus to excel in situations involving standards of excellence. Achievement-value orientations are defined as 'meaningful and affectively charged modes of organizing behavior-principles that guide human conduct. They establish criteria which influence the individual's preferences and goals' (Rosen, 1959: 35). Rosen states, however, that while achievement motivation and value orientations affect individuals' achievements by influencing their need to excel and their willingness to plan and work hard, they 'do not determine the areas in which such excellence and effort takes place' (1959: 57). Unless parents express high educational and occupational goals for their children, Rosen proposes that the other socialisation processes will not necessarily be associated with successful achievement. Unfortunately, studies have rarely included, in detail, all the elements of the achievement syndrome in analyses of children's academic achievement. Instead, research has tended to adopt only certain aspects of the syndrome and related them to achievement scores (e.g. Schwartz, 1971; Evans and Anderson, 1973; Lueptow, 1975; and Anderson and Evans, 1976).

Parents' achievement value orientation is a further dimension, suggested by a consideration of the achievement syndrome, for possible inclusion in the ideal-type definition. In an investigation of relations between family interaction, values and achievement, Strodtbeck (1958) isolated two value scales: independence of family and mastery. The independence of family scale, which is assessed by items such as 'Even when teen-agers get married, their main loyalty still belongs to their fathers and mothers', is similar to a value scale developed by Rosen and named individualistic-collectivistic value orientations. When Strodtbeck combined the independence of family and mastery scales, in an analysis involving Italian and Jewish families, he found that fathers of over-achieving boys had higher value scores than fathers of under-achieving boys. In an investigation including nine value orientations, Schwartz (1971) observed few significant relations between values and achievement measures, but did find that orientation to family authority, which is similar to Rosen's individualistic-collectivistic orientation, was related to academic achievement. In an attempt to maintain some continuity with the achievement syndrome research and from the findings of prior investigations, individualistic-collectivistic value orientation was included as a dimension of the ideal type.

Thus, the ideal-typical academically oriented family operating in an English-language social context is defined, for the present study, as a family that: expresses strong achievement orientations, exerts strong press for English, stresses press for independence, has individualistic rather than collectivistic achievement-value orientations, and has high educational and occupational aspirations for its children. The assessment of academically oriented families is discussed in the following section of the chapter, which examines the measures used in the study.

Measures

Family environment schedule

A new semi-structured interview schedule was constructed to assess the dimensions of the academically oriented family. The schedule was a development from a number of previous questionnaires. In an investigation of relations between family environments and measures of academic achievement, Dave (1963) constructed a schedule to assess six press variables, with each press variable defined by a number of process characteristics. For example, one of the press variables is labelled achievement press, and consists of seven process characteristics: parental aspirations for the education of the child, parents' own aspirations, parents' interest in academic achievement, social press for academic achievement, standards of reward for educational attainment, knowledge of the educational progress of the child, and preparation and planning for the attainment of educational goals. In the complete schedule there are twenty-one process characteristics and interviewers are provided with a nine-point rating scale for each characteristic. Scores on the six press variables are obtained by averaging the ratings on the relevant process characteristics.

Using the same sample of students as Dave and essentially the same set of questions, Wolf (1964) identified three family environment variables that were hypothesised to be related to children's intelligence test performance. Thirteen process characteristics are used in the Wolf version of the schedule to assess the three press variables and interviewers are provided with seven-point scales to rate the characteristics. Scores for the three press variables are obtained by summing the ratings on the relevant characteristics. The schedules developed for these two studies represented an important advance in the measurement of family learning environments and they have been adopted in a number of studies within different national settings. By using such broad rating scales the schedules are particularly subject, however, to the effects of 'experimenter expectancies' (e.g. see criticisms of the methodology by Longstreth, 1978; and Wolff, 1978). Commencing with the Dave-Wolf framework, a more structured schedule was devised by Marjoribanks (1972a, 1974b) for an investigation involving Canadian families, and refined later for a study of Australian children (Marjoribanks, 1978a, 1979c). The structured measure consisted of eight press variables, with each press variable defined by process characteristics. Questions were designed to assess each characteristic and generally a six-point rating scale was devised for each question. The score for each environmental characteristic was obtained by adding the scores on the relevant environmental items, while each press variable was the sum of the scores on the relevant environmental characteristics. Such refinements do not, of course, eliminate completely interviewer bias, nor overcome possible discrepancies between respondents' 'true' answers and those supplied to interviewers. It was considered, however, that by imposing more structure on the previous methodologies, some of the restrictions of open-ended interviews, such as interviewer bias, might be reduced. A more valid assessment of family environments would, of course, be achieved by using a combination of interviews and observation techniques. For the present investigation of families from six ethclasses, however, the adoption of observation methods would have required an investment in research resources that was beyond the scope of the study. Thus, for the analysis of families the schedule shown in Appendix A was constructed and used in interviews with parents.

Final scales for the environment dimensions were constructed using factor-scaling techniques (see Armor, 1974), in which principal component analysis was used to examine responses to the questionnaire items. The five hypothesised dimensions were extracted from the analysis. After eliminating those items in the five factors with small factor loadings ($\leqslant 0.40$), the remaining items were refactored to maximise the theta reliability estimates of the final environment scales. Family environment scores for each child were obtained by adding the scores on those items making up each of the five dimensions. Theta reliability estimates of the final scales were greater than 0.75. In the achievement-orientation scale were the questions: How much time do you think a 10- or 11-year-old should spend doing homework or schoolwork at home? How much time do parents expect their child to devote to homework or schoolwork at home? How often do parents praise their child for work done at school? How often do parents discuss their child's progress at school? What level of education did most of the parents' close friends achieve? and Do parents know what topic their child is studying in, say, arithmetic or English at school? The press for English dimension consists of items of the form: How often would you help your child with English grammar (e.g. tell the child how to construct sentences, when to use certain words)? How particular would you say you are about the way the child speaks English (correct grammar, good vocabulary)? How often is English spoken in the home? How many books in English do parents read in a month? When the child was small, how often did the parents read to her/him in English? How often do the parents listen to the child read to them in English? and How many books does the child bring home from the library each month? Parents' press for independence was assessed using ten items in which parents indicated the age they would allow their child to undertake certain activities. The individualistic-collectivistic achievement-value scale consists of items similar to those used by Strodtbeck (1958) to assess his 'independence of family' scale: Even when a boy (girl) gets married, his (her) main loyalty still belongs to his (her) parents; When the time comes for a son (daughter) to take a job, he (she) should try and stay near his (her) parents, even if it means giving up a good job opportunity; and Nothing in life is worth the sacrifice of moving away from one's parents. The parents' aspirations scale includes items of the form: How much education do you want your child to receive? How much education do you really expect your child to receive? How long have parents had the expectations about their child's education? What kind of job would parents really like their child to have? and How long have parents had these expectations about their child's future occupation?

As well as obtaining information on the five ideal-type dimensions, the environment schedule was also used to collect data on variables such as: social-status, ethnic group membership, parents' perceptions of their satisfaction with the school attended by their 11-year-old child, and parents' concern for the provision of bilingual education in schools. The social-status and ethnic group data were used to check information collected from school records and to assist in the classification of families into ethclasses. Research investigating relations between parents' satisfaction with schooling and children's school attainments has produced inconsistent and inconclusive findings (see Acland, 1975). In the early planning of the study it was thought that parents' satisfaction with school might be an appropriate ideal-type dimension. But while research provides no reliable indication of the nature of associations between children's achievement and parents' satisfaction, there is also no clear understanding of how other family environment dimensions are related to satisfaction measures. For example, parents may create a highly achievement-oriented family environment as a reaction to their dissatisfaction with their child's school, or they may relax their efforts within the home because they are so satisfied with what the school appears to be accomplishing. Because of such possibilities, it was decided to analyse parents' satisfactions separately and to test a proposition generated from Acland's analysis: that the relationship between parents' satisfaction with school and children's academic achievement varies at different levels of children's intelligence and their attitudes to school.

Australian schools, with large enrolments of non-English-speaking children, are confronted with the challenge of constructing a curriculum that will be related to the successful achievement of those children. A major concern of educators is to what extent bilingual programmes should be developed. As part of the present research, questions were placed in the interview schedule in order to gauge parents' initial reactions to the possibility of schools offering bilingual-type courses. Analyses of these questions are presented in the final chapter, when some policy implications of the research are discussed.

Therefore, the family environment schedule designed for the study assesses the five dimensions of an academically oriented family: achievement orientations, press for independence, press for English, individualistic-collectivistic achievement-value orientations, and educational and occupational aspirations, as well as measures of parents' satisfaction with schooling, parents' concern for the teaching of bilingual-type curriculum, and social-structural characteristics of families. Interviewing in the homes was conducted by experienced government social-survey interviewers who were able to communicate in the primary language of the family.

School-related attitudes

In a theory linking social organisation and social personality, Thomas and Znaniecki (1958) propose that in the field of social reality an effect, whether individual or social, always has a composite cause. It is claimed that the cause contains the subjective social-psychological elements of social reality (called attitudes) and the objective social elements that impose themselves upon individuals and provoke their reactions (social values). They suggest that there can be no change of social reality which is not the common effect of pre-existing social values and individual attitudes acting upon them, nor any change of individual consciousness that is not the common effect of pre-existing attitudes and social values acting upon them. The framework developed by Thomas and Znaniecki is reflected in the model presented in Figure 1.2, in which the academic achievement of children is shown to be related to both family environments and school-related attitudes. That is, if the family learning environment is considered to represent a set of social values which may arouse intellectual reactions in children, then it is proposed that the associations between family environments and children's achievements vary at different levels of children's school attitudes. Similarly, it is proposed that relations between children's school attitudes and their achievements vary at different family environment levels. As Thomas (1966: 277) suggests, 'the cause of a value or an attitude is never an attitude or value alone, but always a combination of an attitude and a value'. The important role of attitudes in the Thomas and Znaniecki conceptual framework is mirrored in many other social-psychological theories of behaviour. As a result, it was decided to include a measure of children's school-related attitudes in the analysis, in particular to test the proposition that relations between children's school attitudes and their achievements vary at different levels of family environments.

The school-related attitudes were measured using a Likert-type questionnaire, adapted from a schedule developed originally by the National Foundation for Educational Research in England and used in a number of studies of streaming in English schools (Barker Lunn, 1969, 1970; Ferri, 1971; and Newbold, 1977). In a description of the questionnaire, in which reliability and validity data are presented, Barker Lunn (1970) indicates that the initial items were obtained from statements made by children who were discussing attitudes related to school. From a principal component analysis of the responses to the items shown in the questionnaire in Appendix B, seven attitude scales were generated. The following list includes the labels used for the scales, with some of the sample items provided to indicate the nature of the scales: (a) enthusiasm for school (I am sorry when school is over for the day, I would leave school tomorrow if I could, school is boring), (b) enthusiasm for class membership, which assesses the favourableness or otherwise of being a member of a particular class in the school (of all the classes in this school my class is the nicest of all, I would rather be in my class than in any other, I hate being in the class I'm in now), (c) dislike for disruptive behaviour (I dislike children who are noisy in class, I like fooling about in this class, when the teacher goes out of the room I fool about), (d) relationship with teacher (I get on well with my teacher, our teacher treats us as if we were babies, my teacher is nice to me), (e) academic self-image, which reflects self-image in terms of schoolwork

(I'm useless at schoolwork, when we have work to do I get very good marks, I think that I am pretty good at schoolwork), (f) social adjustment in school, which assesses children's ability to get on well with peers (I have no friends who I like very much in this school, I wish there were nicer children in this class, generally I have no one to play with at lunch time), and (g) achievement orientation (I work and try very hard in school, doing well at school is most important to me, and I would like to be one of the cleverest students in the school).

Thus a wide range of school-related attitudes is assessed by the schedule. In the administration of the questionnaire, I read each item to the children in their classrooms, in order to minimise, as far as possible, any difficulties associated with understanding the meaning of the questions. When scores on the seven subscales were factor analysed, using principal component analysis, two factors were identified. The first factor had a theta reliability estimate of 0.80, consisted of twenty-eight items and assessed an affective component of school-related attitudes. Labelled, 'affective commitment to school', the factor loaded on the scales: enthusiasm for school, enthusiasm for class, dislike for disruptive behaviour, and positive relationship with the teacher. (The items from the questionnaire used in assessing affective commitment to school are: 1, 2, 3, 5, 8, 9, 10, 11, 13, 17, 18, 20, 21, 22, 28, 30, 34, 35, 37, 42, 43, 45, 47, 49, 51, 52, 54, and 57.)

A cognitive-behavioural component of school attitudes was measured by the second factor, which consisted of nineteen items and had a theta reliability estimate of 0.76. The factor was labelled 'academic adjustment to school' and loaded on the scales: academic self-image, achievement orientation, and social adjustment to school. (Items used to measure the factor are: 4, 7, 12, 15, 23, 24, 26, 27, 28, 29, 32, 40, 41, 46, 53, 55, 58, 59, and 60.)

Cognitive performance

The difficulties associated with testing children, in general, and children from different cultural groups, in particular, have been well documented. A test of academic achievement represents a social situation reflecting a set of special relationships between the participants. As Riessman (1974: 207) indicates, 'Children from different cultural backgrounds respond very differently to clinical situations and the idea of being tested or evaluated.' In an attempt to create as uniform test-taking situations as possible, I administered the testing programme within classrooms with the assistance of one other researcher who was involved in working with elementary-school children and teachers. Such an approach to testing would not be satisfactory if the test scores were to be used, in some way, for judging individual children. It was felt, however, that by adopting a series of precautionary measures, social situations were created that allowed the generation of test results that were valid for the analysis of ethclass group differences in children's performances.

The Raven's Progressive Matrices measure was used to assess intellectual ability as it appears to have a greater degree of cultural neutrality than most other measures of intelligence. Tests devised by the Australian Council for Educational Research were adopted to assess achievement in mathematics, word knowledge and word comprehension. The mathematics test is labelled the Class Achievement Test in Mathematics (1976 edition) and consists of forty-five multiple-choice items assessing ten content categories: counting and place value, whole numbers, money, common fractions, decimal fractions, spatial relations, length, area, volume and capacity, mass and weight, and time. Also, each item is classified into one of four relatively distinct areas which describe, in general, the nature of the thinking processes required to meet the item objective. These four areas are labelled: knowledge (requiring the child to have mastered the terminology, symbols and many of the factual relationships of mathematics), computation (concerned with the child's ability to perform recognised mathematical processes accurately), application (assesses the child's ability to apply his/her knowledge, skill and understanding of mathematics), and understanding (requiring children to identify principles and relationships and to reach valid generalisations). Word knowledge and word comprehension were measured using the Primary Reading Survey Tests (1976). Each word knowledge item attempts to assess the understanding of a common meaning of a word supplied. Children are required to choose the word closest in meaning to the given word from a set of three or four plausible choices. In the reading comprehension test there are a number of prose and dialogue passages from a variety of subject areas. Questions are designed to measure the student's comprehension of facts, inferences, implications and underlying assumptions. The testing programme and the interviewing of parents were conducted towards the end of the school year.

Thus the study primarily examines relations between performance on tests of mathematics, word knowledge and word comprehension, and measures of intelligence, affective commitment to school and academic adjustment to school, at different levels of parents': press for English, press for independence, individualistic-collectivistic value orientations, achievement orientations, and aspirations. In the following chapters relationships among these variables are investigated.

3

Environment and Achievement: Group Differences

Although there have been many investigations of social group differences in children's achievements, findings from the research remain inconsistent and inconclusive. There is little agreement, for example, on whether parents create different learning environments for girls and boys, or to what extent girls and boys differ on measures of cognitive performance and affective characteristics (see Maccoby, 1966; Butler and Kellmer Pringle, 1967; Deutsch, 1967; Hutt, 1972; Alexander and Eckland, 1974; Maccoby and Jacklin, 1974; Hout and Morgan, 1975; and Epstein and McPartland, 1977). Also, the controversies generated from studies such as those of Jensen (1969, 1973a, 1973b), Eysenck (1971, 1973), Shockley (1971a, 1971b), and Herrnstein (1973) show that we continue to have a limited understanding of social-status and ethnic group differences in children's achievements. In part, the research remains equivocal because it has tended to rely on the use of global measures of children's social environments. Also, investigations of social group differences in children's performances have generally failed to examine relations between refined measures of children's family environments and academic achievement, at varying levels of other person characteristics such as intelligence and school-related attitudes. In the present chapter, relations between the variables shown in Figure 3.1 are analysed, in an attempt to overcome some of the restrictions of previous investigations of sex and ethclass group differences in children's academic achievement.

As part of the statistical investigation in the present chapter, and in later chapters, a variation of multiple regression analysis is adopted. Regression surfaces are plotted, using raw regression weights generated from regression equations containing quadratic terms, to test for non-linearity, and product terms, to test for interactions. That is, regression models of the following form are examined:

$$Z = aX + bY + cXY + dX^2 + eY^2 + \text{constant}$$

where Z represents measures of academic achievement and X and Y are measures of children's social environments and individual characteristics. The letters *a* to *e* stand for raw regression weights. Regression surface analysis allows a figural presentation of relations between variables, and it is a useful methodology for testing an interactionism framework of analysis.

Because simple random samples were not selected, the design effects for the raw regression weights are estimated throughout the analysis and the significance levels of the weights recalculated (see p. 29). Typically, adjustments to the significance levels led to a reduction in the number of regression weights remaining significant. Often the adjusted standard errors showed that the interaction and curvilinear terms were not significant. In such cases, a second stage of the regression analysis was conducted and variables no longer having associations with children's achievement were deleted from the regression models. In the second analysis, the design effects were again estimated, if necessary, and the significance levels of regression weights adjusted further.

Regression surfaces are constructed in the following section of the chapter, where sex-group differences in the relations shown in Figure 3.1 are examined.

Environment, individual characteristics and achievement: sex differences

Studies of the correlates of children's achievements that have overcome restrictions of prior investigations, by including refined family environment measures, have often been limited either by their use of small samples or samples of only girls or boys. For example, in a set of investigations of relations between the quality of stimulation found in the homes of infants and performance on cognitive measures, Bradley and Caldwell (1976, 1977) and Elardo *et al.* (1975, 1977) sampled approximately eighty infants, with few of the analyses incorporating an examination of sex-group differences. Research generated from Bloom's (1964) conceptual position (see p. 000) has often used smaller samples. Dave (1963) and Wolf (1964) observed the same 11-year-olds, thirty-two girls and twenty-eight boys, while in an investigation of family environments and the affective characteristics of 11-year-olds, Weiss (1969, 1974) sampled twenty-nine girls and twenty-seven boys. Adaptations of the Dave-Wolf family schedule have been used in studies of: 10-year-old Trinidadian children, thirty girls and thirty boys, by Dyer (1967); twenty-six American

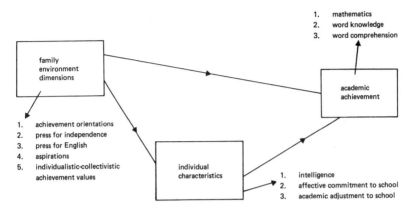

Figure 3.1 Correlates of children's academic achievement

kindergarten children by Levine *et al.* (1972); 11-year-olds in Dublin, thirty girls and thirty boys, by Kellaghan (1977), and grade-nine girls, from fifty white and fifty black-American families, by Trotman (1977, 1978). Further refinements of the environment measures were made in analyses: by Mosychuk (1969) of 100 10-year-old boys from Western Canada; by Keeves (1972) of 215 12-year-olds from the Australian Capital Territory; by Marjoribanks (1972*b*, 1976*b*) of 185 11-year-old boys from Ontario in Canada; and by Marjoribanks (1978*a*, 1978*b*) of 12-year-olds, 120 girls and 130 boys, from Australian rural towns.

While such studies represent significant advances in the development of family environment schedules, the validity of some of the findings is restricted by possible statistical errors associated with using particularly small samples. In the ensuing analysis, 414 and 436 11-year-old girls and boys, respectively, are used in an examination of the following questions:

1. Are there sex-related differences in scores on the measures of cognitive performance and attitudes to school?
2. Do parents create different family learning environments for girls and boys?
3. Are there sex-related differences in associations between family environments, children's individual characteristics, and academic achievement?

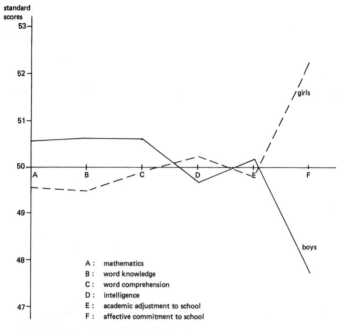

A :   mathematics
B :   word knowledge
C :   word comprehension
D :   intelligence
E :   academic adjustment to school
F :   affective commitment to school

Figure 3.2   Profiles of achievement, intelligence and attitude scores
for girls and boys

Sex-related differences in cognitive and attitude scores

In Figure 3.2 the cognitive and attitude scores have been standardised, with a mean of fifty and a standard deviation of ten, calculated
over the total sample. A similar standardisation of scores is adopted
throughout the study when other profiles are presented. After making
allowances for the design effects of the samples, the only significant
group differences in Figure 3.2 relate to children's affective commitment to school. The affective commitment measure has four subscales: enthusiasm for school, dislike for disruptive behaviour,
positive relationship with teacher, and enthusiasm for class. Girls'
mean scores on the first two subscales are significantly higher than
the boys' scores, while differences on the remaining scales are not
significant. The general lack of sex-related cognitive differences suggests support for the proposition that, by the end of elementary
school, there are few significant differences in the mean cognitive
performances of girls and boys.

Sex-group differences in family learning environments

It is often proposed that parents may structure differential learning environments for girls and boys (e.g. Moore, 1967, 1968; Hoffman, 1972; Hutt, 1972; Lee and Gropper, 1974; Hout and Morgan, 1975; and Epstein and McPartland, 1977). In Figure 3.3, the profiles show, however, that in the present study press for dependence is the only family dimension on which parents differentiate between girls and boys. The higher mean score for girls indicates that parents allow boys to pursue independently a set of activities at earlier ages than they do for girls. Throughout the analysis, the press for independence scale is scored with a high value, indicating that parents do not encourage independent activities by their children. For ease of interpretation the scale has been renamed press for dependence.

Thus, the profiles in Figures 3.2 and 3.3 show that the patterns of mean scores for girls and boys are very similar. For 11-year-old children, these findings provide little support for propositions sug-

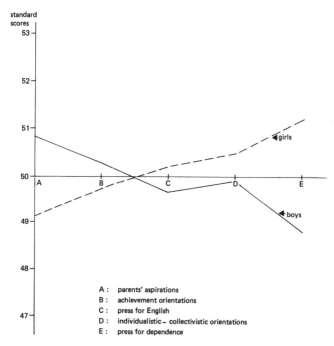

A : parents' aspirations
B : achievement orientations
C : press for English
D : individualistic – collectivistic orientations
E : press for dependence

Figure 3.3 Profiles of family dimension scores for girls and boys

TABLE 3.1 *Relations between environment dimensions, attitudes and cognitive performance*

	Mathematics	Word knowledge	Word comprehension	Intelligence	Academic adjustment	Affective commitment
Aspirations (boys)	0.12**[a]	0.10*	0.10*	0.08	0.10*	0.07
Aspirations (girls)	0.07	0.06	0.03	0.07	0.12*	0.06
Achievement orientations (boys)	0.15**	0.25**	0.22**	0.10*	0.02	0.06
Achievement orientations (girls)	0.20**	0.31**	0.35**	0.13*	0.01	0.06
Press for English (boys)	0.20**	0.36**	0.22**	0.12*	0.03	0.05
Press for English (girls)	0.14**	0.26**	0.34**	0.12*	0.03	0.09
Value orientations[b] (boys)	0.14**	0.28**	0.26**	0.08	-0.05	0.02
Value orientations (girls)	0.14**	0.28**	0.27**	0.06	-0.05	0.04
Press for dependence (boys)	-0.12*	-0.26**	-0.20**	-0.07	0.08	0.01
Press for dependence (girls)	-0.18**	-0.27**	-0.20**	-0.10	0.06	0.03
Intelligence (boys)	0.53**	0.31**	0.32**	—	0.12*	0.07
Intelligence (girls)	0.57**	0.24**	0.19**	—	0.06	0.09
Academic adjustment (boys)	0.12*	0.16**	0.14**	0.12*	—	0.40**
Academic adjustment (girls)	0.10*	0.19**	0.18**	0.06	—	0.50**
Affective commitment (boys)	0.13**	0.11*	0.13**	0.07	0.40**	—
Affective commitment (girls)	0.09	0.09	0.09	0.09	0.50**	—
Family environment index (boys)	0.24**	0.38**	0.32**	0.15**	0.03	0.07
Family environment index (girls)	0.25**	0.42**	0.39**	0.15**	0.01	0.08
Social status index (boys)	0.17**	0.27**	0.20**	0.11*	0.01	0.05
Social status index (girls)	0.19**	0.34**	0.34**	0.13**	0.01	0.07

[a] Coefficients for boys are uppermost in each pair while those for girls are below
[b] High score indicates individualistic value orientations
* $p < 0.05$
** $p < 0.01$

gesting that girls and boys differ in mean school performance or that parents create different sex-related family learning environments.

Environment, intelligence and achievement: sex-related differences

The first examination of the associations between family environment, intelligence and academic achievement, for girls and boys, involves an analysis of zero-order correlations. In Table 3.1, the correlations show that the patterns of relations for girls and boys are very similar. Typically, the family environment dimensions and cognitive scores have low to moderate associations, with the relations between the dimensions and word scores being stronger than those between the environment and measures of intelligence and mathematics. These latter findings support previous research showing that environmental measures are more strongly related to verbal achievement than to non-verbal performances. When the environment dimensions are combined into an index—with a high value reflecting a combination of strong achievement orientations, high educational and occupational aspirations, individualistic value orientations, strong press for dependence, and high press for English—the index has moderate associations with academic achievement scores and low concurrent validities in relation to intelligence. A social-status index consisting of an equally weighted composite of father's occupation and the education of the mother and the father, has low to moderate relations to the cognitive scores. Correlations between social status and girls' word-test scores approach the value of 0.35, which is often found in studies investigating social-status correlates of children's achievements. In general, the intelligence scores have stronger associations with mathematics than with the word-test scores, while social status and family environment have stronger links with word-test scores than with mathematics performance. These differences are likely to reflect, in part, the ethnic nature of the sample. In Chapter 5, relations between family environment, intelligence and academic achievement within the different ethclasses are further explored.

From previous research there is no clear indication of how intelligence and measures of family social environment, when considered together, are related to children's achievements. It is sometimes proposed that social status continues to have a strong association with academic achievement, even when measures of intelligence are controlled (e.g. Banks, 1976; Gordon, 1976; Featherman and Carter, 1976; and Kerckhoff and Campbell, 1977). Other researchers suggest that social status has few or no links with

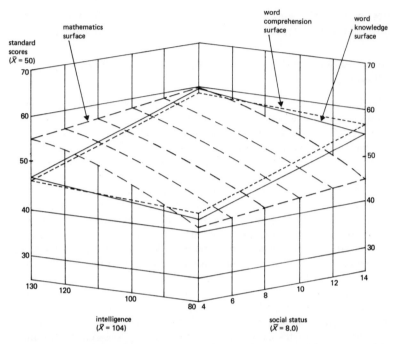

Figure 3.4 Fitted-achievement scores in relation to social status and intelligence: girls' scores

the academic performance of children of equal ability (see Alexander *et al.*, 1975; Sewell and Hauser, 1975, 1976; Wilson and Portes, 1975; Spencer, 1976; and Williams, 1976). For a more complete analysis of relations between social environment measures, intelligence and academic achievement, regression surfaces were constructed to examine associations between academic performance and intelligence at different levels of both social status and family environment, for girls and boys. The surfaces in Figure 3.4 represent the regression-fitted relations between social status and academic achievement at different levels of the intelligence test scores. Surfaces for the boys are not plotted, as they do not differ significantly from those of the girls. In the surfaces the achievement scores have been standardised with a mean of fifty and a standard deviation of ten. At each level of intelligence, the regression surfaces for the word test scores show that substantial increases in social status are associated with sizeable increments in word performance. But at each social-status level, large increases in intelligence scores are related to extremely modest increases in word achievement. As the social-status level changes, for example, from a low of four to a high of fourteen, the regression-estimated word knowledge and word comprehension values increase by approximately thirteen points at each level of intelligence. And, at each social-status level, increases in intelligence scores from 80 to 130 are associated with increments of approximately five and four points in the word knowledge and word comprehension values, respectively.

For mathematics, the regression surface indicates a slightly negative curvilinear relation between intelligence and mathematics achievement at each social-status level. As the status scores increase from four to fourteen, the regression-estimated mathematics values increase by five points at each intelligence level, while at each social-status level increases in intelligence from 80 to 130 are associated with an overall increment of fourteen points.

Clearly, the surfaces show the differential relations between the word and mathematics scores and measures of social status and intelligence. But social-status indices provide only an approximate assessment of family learning environments. Therefore, in a further attempt to understand the relations between intelligence and academic achievement, another set of regression surfaces is presented in Figure 3.5. These surfaces show the regression-fitted associations between the family learning environment index (see p. 50) and achievement, at different intelligence levels. The girls' surfaces are similar to those for the boys and have not been plotted. As in Figure 3.4, the sufaces indicate that at each environment level, increases in intelligence are associated more strongly with increments in mathematics performance than with word-test scores. Also, at each intelligence level the increases in word-test scores associated with increments in the academic orientation of families are greater than the corresponding changes in mathematics performance.

For both girls and boys, the regression surface analyses show that at different intelligence levels, quite sizeable increases in social-environment measures are associated with moderate to large increments in the achievement scores. The shapes of the surfaces also indicate, however, that small increases in the achievement orientation of families are related to quite modest increments in children's academic performances. If it is assumed that intelligence scores represent, in part, the results of past environmental influences and also reflect previous academic performance, then the surfaces indicate that modest changes in family environments may be related to very small variations in children's achievements. Unless educational policies adopt bold programmes for assisting families, then these initial findings suggest that the policies may not be rewarded by particularly significant gains in children's performances.

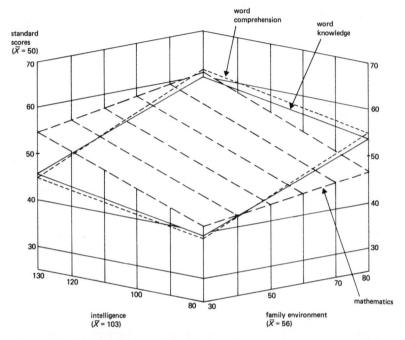

Figure 3.5   Fitted-achievement scores in relation to family environment and intelligence: boys' scores

Social status, environment and academic achievement

Although the regression surfaces that have been presented examine, separately, social status and the family environment dimensions, it is an assumption of the present study that family environments are an integral part of the work and community situation of children. The analysis accepts Halsey's (1975: 17) caveat that

> it is essential to insist that the effect of class on educational experience is not to be thought of as one factor from which parental attitudes and motivations to succeed in education are independent. A theory which explains educational achievement as the outcome of a set of individual attributes has lost the meaning of those structural forces which we know as class.

Interrelationships between social status, the family environment

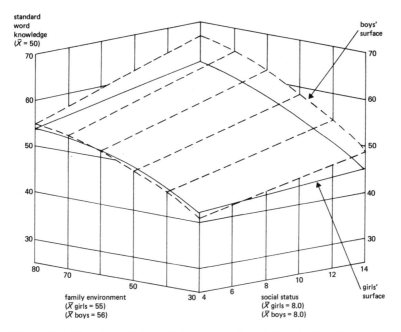

Figure 3.6 Fitted-word knowledge scores in relation to family environment and social status: girls and boys

index and children's achievements were investigated using regression surface analysis. In Figure 3.6, the surfaces that show associations with word knowledge have been presented, as they reflect the curvature of the regression planes for the other achievement scores. The shapes of the surfaces show that family environment has a slightly negative curvilinear association with the performance scores. Also, the product term in the regressions is significant, indicating that the interaction between family environment and social status is related to children's performance. The influence of the interaction term on the shapes of the surfaces is most noticeable at high levels of environment and social status. These findings discount research results suggesting that socialisation processes within families are related to children's achievements independently of social-status conditions. For example, at a high environment level of eighty, the estimated-word knowledge scores for girls and boys are fifty-three and fifty-four respectively, at a low social-status level of four. The corresponding regression-estimated values at a high status level of fourteen are sixty-one and sixty-seven. These initial investigations of sex-related differences in children's performances show that regression surface analysis provides a useful way of displaying some of the complexities of the relations between social environments and children's school outcomes.

Environment, school-related attitudes and achievement:
sex-related differences

In Figure 3.1, school-related attitudes are also included in the analysis of relations between family environments and children's achievement. Research investigating associations between attitudes to school and academic performance has produced equivocal findings. For example, McBee and Duke (1960), Brodie (1964), Finger and Schlesser (1968), Kahn (1969), Williams (1970), Keeves (1972, 1974), Husén *et al.* (1974), Johnson (1974), Aiken (1976), and Marjoribanks (1976c, 1977a) have observed low to moderate significant relations between school attitude scores and measures of achievement. Malpass (1953) found that attitudes were associated with achievement when it was assessed by end-of-term grades, but not related to achievement when measured by standardised tests. Aiken and Dreger (1961) found that attitudes were a significant predictor of mathematics achievement for females but not for males, while Jackson and Lahaderne (1967) and Goldfried and D'Zurilla (1973) observed no significant links between attitudes and achievement. Similarly, in a study of American high school students, Fennema and Sherman (1977: 68) concluded that 'was little direct evidence that attitude towards success in mathematics is an important variable influencing mathematics achievement of high school girls'. But Levin (1976: 285) proposes that

> educational programs that focus on student attitudes may be able to compensate for 'disadvantages' in socioeconomic background. Indeed, this tentative interpretation argues ... that, these background factors now appear to have much of their direct effects not on achievement, but on attitude, and through attitude, on achievement.

After reviewing studies showing little or no associations between attitudes and achievement, Jackson (1968) claims that no apparent relationship exists between attitudes and achievement and that the relation is the same for girls and boys, and does not depend on whether achievement is assessed by course grades or test scores. Similarly, Good *et al.* (1975: 198) propose that 'simple one-to-one relationships between global attitudes that children hold toward school and achievement on standardized tests do not appear to exist'.

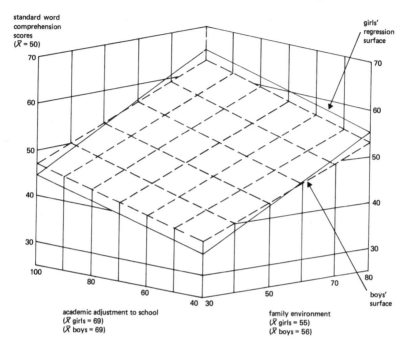

Figure 3.7 Fitted-word comprehension scores in relation to family environment and academic adjustment to school: girls and boys

Inconsistencies in the research are related, in part, to the failure of most of the studies to include in their analyses an examination of children's social environments. Lavin's (1965: 100) conclusion is still applicable, that the 'disappointing state of affairs' in research relating affective characteristics and children's performances may be due to the circumstance that virtually all studies 'conceive of the individual as if he were operating in a social vacuum'. Also, Getzels (1969: 100) notes that such research 'might be more powerful if the social setting in which educational performance takes place were conceptualized and used as a significant variable with which personality interacts'.

The zero-order correlations in Table 3.1 show that the two attitude scales have negligible or low significant associations with the cognitive scores. Relations between academic adjustment to school and achievement are similar, for girls and boys, while the affective commitment to school scale is associated only with boys' performances. In Figure 3.7, the regression surfaces are representative of those situations in which both attitudes and family environments are associated with achievement. Product and curvilinear terms were not significant in any of the regression models including attitude scores. From an analysis of all the regression surfaces involving attitudes, the following propositions are suggested: (a) for boys, at each family environment level increases in affective commitment and academic orientation to school are associated with low to modest increments in academic achievement, (b) for girls, increments in academic orientation to school are associated with small increases in academic achievement at each family environment level, and (c) for girls and boys, at each level of school-related attitudes, increases in family environment scores are related to modest increases in achievement scores.

Typically, the findings in this section of the chapter show few sex-related differences in the relations between family environment, intelligence, school-related attitudes and academic achievement. But as Walberg and Marjoribanks (1976: 527) have suggested, 'correlational or causal relationships established for one group may not hold for other times, social classes, ethnic groups, or countries'. Therefore, in the following part of the chapter, relations between the variables shown in Figure 3.1 are examined with the total sample divided into ethclass groups. As the sample sizes within some ethclasses would become too small for valid analyses if divided by sex, the following investigations generally are based on pooled data for girls and boys. Although the previous results indicate relatively few gender-related differences, the failure to test for sex differences within ethclasses is a restriction of the study.

Environment, individual characteristics and achievement: ethclass group differences

A general theoretical position has been proposed by Ferguson (1954, 1956) and Lesser (1976), suggesting that if children from different cultural groups are found to be characterised by different patterns of cognitive scores, then the groups are characterised by distinct patterns of learning environments. In part, the present section of the chapter is a test of the theoretical position as the following questions are examined:

1. Are there ethclass group differences in scores on measures of cognitive performance and attitudes to school?
2. Are there ethclass group differences in the family learning environments created by parents?

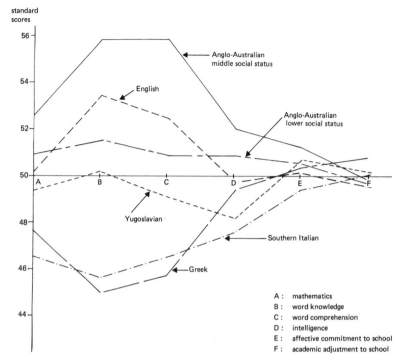

standard
scores

Figure 3.8 Profiles of cognitive and attitude scores for each ethclass group

3. To what extent is the learning environment of the family related to ethclass group differences in children's performances?

Ethclass group differences in cognitive and attitude scores

The profiles of cognitive and attitude mean scores for the children from each ethclass are shown in Figure 3.8. After making adjustments for the design effects of the samples, the following significant group differences were observed:

1. For mathematics, the Anglo-Australian middle social-status mean score is higher than those of the Southern Italian and Greek children, while the Anglo-Australian lower social-status mean performance is higher than that for the Southern Italian children.

2. The Anglo-Australian middle social-status mean word knowledge value is higher than the means of other groups, except for the English children. Anglo-Australian lower social-status and English group mean word knowledge scores are higher than those of the

Southern Italian and Greek children, while the Yugoslavian value is higher than that of the Greek children.

3. For word comprehension, the Anglo-Australian middle social-status mean is higher than the performances of other groups except for that of the English children, while the Anglo-Australian lower social-status and English means are higher than those of the Southern Italian and Greek children.

4. The mean intelligence score of the Anglo-Australian middle social-status children is higher than the mean scores of the Southern Italian and Yugoslavian children, while the Anglo-Australian lower social-status mean intelligence score is higher than the Southern Italian mean score.

5. Children from the ethclass groups do not differ significantly in their mean affective commitment or academic adjustment to school scores.

Thus the findings relating to the first question show that there are ethclass group differences in the cognitive measures, with the largest mean differences occurring in performances on the word measures. In multiple regression models, where the ethclass group data formed a set of mutually exclusive categories and the cognitive scores the criterion variables, ethclass was associated with 2, 4, 12 and 11 per cent of the variance in intelligence, mathematics, word knowledge and word comprehension, respectively.

Ethclass group differences in family learning environments

In Figure 3.9, the profiles of family environment dimensions for each ethclass are shown with the following significant differences in group mean scores being present:

1. For parents' aspirations, the Greek mean is higher than those of the Yugoslavians and the three English-speaking groups, while the Southern Italian and Yugoslavian mean scores are higher than those of the Anglo-Australian lower status and English scores. Anglo-Australian middle social-status families have higher mean aspirations than the Anglo-Australian lower status families.

2. The mean achievement-orientation value for the Anglo-Australian middle social-status group is higher than the means of all the other groups, while the scores of the Anglo-Australian lower social-status, Greek, English and Yugoslavian groups are higher than the mean achievement-orientation value of the Southern Italian families.

3. For press for English, the scores of the Anglo-Australian middle social-status and English groups are higher than those of the other

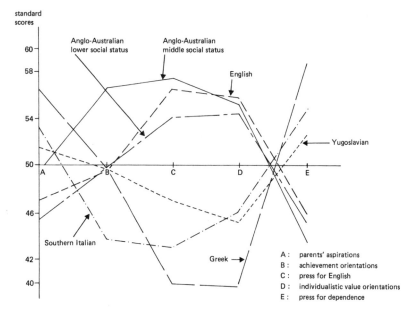

Figure 3.9 Profiles of family environment dimensions for each ethclass

four groups, while the Anglo-Australian lower status group mean is greater than that of the Yugoslavian, Greek and Southern Italian families.

4. A high value orientation score indicates that parents express individualistic value orientations rather than collectivistic orientations. The mean value orientation scores of the three English-speaking ethclass groups are higher than the means of the remaining three ethclasses, while the Southern Italian and Yugoslavian scores are more individualistic than that of Greek families.

5. The press for dependence mean score of Greek families is higher than the means of the other ethclass groups, indicating that Greek parents allow less independence for their 11-year-old children. Also the Southern Italian and Yugoslavian means are higher than those of the three English-speaking groups.

Typically, differences in levels of the family dimension scores of English-speaking groups are characterised by relatively: strong press for English, weak press for dependence, individualistic value orientations, moderate to low aspirations, and moderate to high achievement orientations. In contrast, the Greek and Southern Italian families exhibit lower press for English, stonger press for dependence, more collectivistic value orientations, higher educational-occupational aspirations, and have moderate to lower achievement orientations, while the Yugoslavian profile represents, in general, an intermediate position between the Anglo and non-Anglo groups. Therefore, the findings suggest that families from the three Anglo groups approximate much more closely the ideal-typical definition of an academically oriented family than do non-Anglo group families. An interesting exception from the ideal type is the relation between ethclass group membership and parents' aspirations, with the Greek and Southern Italian families expressing the highest aspirations for their children. Much previous research has observed that parents' aspirations have particularly strong associations with children's cognitive performance (e.g. see Alexander and Eckland, 1974; Alexander *et al.*, 1975; Sewell and Hauser, 1975; Wilson and Portes, 1975; and Marjoribanks, 1977*b*). Generally, such research has been restricted to samples of English-speaking children or to non-English-speaking children being taught in classrooms in the primary language of their family.

If the low associations, in the present study, between parents' aspirations and children's performances (see Table 3.1) are associated with the profiles of family environment dimensions, then the following tentative proposition is suggested: for non-Anglo children being taught in English-speaking contexts, low press for English, high press for dependence, and collectivistic value orientations may act as environmental obstacles restricting high parental aspirations, and in the case of Greek and Yugoslavian families moderate achievement orientations, from being translated into successful children's academic performance.

Perhaps some of the dimensions of the academically oriented family-type act as threshold variables, such that until certain levels of these particular dimensions are attained, other environment measures will have a limited association with children's performances. For example, very low press for English, high press for dependence and strong collectivistic value orientations may, in a sense, encircle a child, preventing other environment dimensions from substantially interacting with the child to influence cognitive performance. Such suggestions may be linked to Lewin's (1935) field theory of behaviour, which proposes that the environment surrounding individuals can be considered as being differentiated into regions. The regions may be defined along a continuum of 'nearness-remoteness' which is an indication of the extent of influence that one environmental region has on another. Also, the boundaries of environment regions may be defined along the continua of 'firm-weak' and 'fluid-rigid'. If boundaries are firm then the environment regions have minimal interaction, but if the boundaries are weak then the regions may exert considerable influence on each other. A fluid region is one that responds quickly to any influence brought to bear upon it, while a rigid medium resists change. In relation to these environmental constructs, the present investigation suggests that regions surrounding Anglo children may be classified as near rather than remote while the boundaries of the regions are more fluid and weak rather than rigid and strong. In contrast, for non-Anglo children within English-speaking contexts, boundaries within a child's family environment space may be more rigid and firmer, and some of the environment regions may be quite remote from the child. Aspects of these propositions are tested in Chapter 5, when regression surfaces are constructed to examine relations between different dimensions of the academically oriented family ideal-type and children's performances, within different ethclasses.

Ethclass, family environment, and children's cognitive performance

A multiple regression model was used to examine the third question, 'to what extent is the learning environment of the family related to ethclass differences in children's performances?' School-related attitudes were not included in the analysis, as the ethclass differences in mean attitude scores were shown not to be significant (p. 60). In the analysis, the unique amount of variance in the cognitive scores that could be associated with ethclass was determined, after accounting for the variance that could be related to the family environment dimensions and to the covariation of ethclass and the environment measures. The findings presented in Table 3.2 show that ethclass has stronger associations with the cognitive scores of girls than of boys, which may indicate that: (a) the meanings attributed to ethclass group membership are more significant for girls than boys, or (b) there are family environment dimensions not included in the present study that are related more strongly to girls' achievement than to boys' cognitive performance. After accounting for the unique relations and the joint associations with the environment, the cognitive scores generally continue to have small but significant associations with ethclass. Exceptions are with boys' intelligence and mathematics scores. The significant joint associations of ethclass and the environment, with the performance scores, may reflect the distinct profiles of family environment scores that are linked to each ethclass. In general, the findings in this section of the chapter provide general

TABLE 3.2 *Relations between ethclass, family dimensions and cognitive performance*

Criterion Predictor variables	Girls		Boys	
	Multiple R	100R^2	Multiple R	100R^2
Intelligence				
Ethclass	0.194	3.76	0.102	1.04[a]
Ethclass + environment	0.230	5.29	0.196	3.84[a]
Family environment	0.139	1.93[a]	0.181	3.28
Unique ethclass		3.36		0.56[a]
Unique environment		1.53[a]		2.80
Joint (ethclass, environment)		0.40[a]		0.48[a]
Mathematics				
Ethclass	0.245	6.00	0.207	4.28
Ethclass + environment	0.292	8.53	0.289	8.35
Family environment	0.241	5.81	0.258	6.66
Unique ethclass		2.72		1.69[a]
Unique environment		2.53		4.07
Joint (ethclass, environment)		3.28		2.77
Word knowledge				
Ethclass	0.456	20.79	0.360	12.96
Ethclass + environment	0.492	24.21	0.456	20.79
Family environment	0.410	16.81	0.411	16.89
Unique ethclass		7.40		3.90
Unique environment		3.42		7.83
Joint (ethclass, environment)		13.39		9.06
Word comprehension				
Ethclass	0.457	20.88	0.291	8.47
Ethclass + environment	0.483	23.33	0.378	14.29
Family environment	0.381	14.52	0.338	11.42
Unique ethclass		8.81		2.87
Unique environment		2.45		5.82
Joint (ethclass, environment)		12.07		5.60

[a] Indicates that coefficient is not significant at 0.05 level. All other coefficients are significant.

support for the proposition that families from different ethclasses create differential learning environments for their children, and that these environments are related to ethclass group differences in children's academic performance.

Perhaps the major implications of the findings in the chapter relate to the suggestion that environment dimensions may be associated with academic achievement in the form of a hierarchy. That is, certain levels of particular environmental dimensions may need to be attained before other family measures, lower in the hierarchy, begin to be associated with children's achievements. If support is provided for the suggestion, then it follows that educators developing supportive programmes for families may need to direct their initial attention to a limited set of environmental circumstances. Also, the different ethclass group patterns of environment and cognitive scores indicate that it must not be assumed that programmes devised to assist families from one particular ethclass can easily be adapted for families in other groups.

The results of the chapter suggest that the definition of an academically oriented family provides a set of significant dimensions for examining social group differences in the cultural capital of families. Restricting analyses to the broad dimensions, however, does not generate an understanding of how families from different ethclasses differ in the structure of the environment dimensions. In the following chapter a more detailed analysis of ethclass group differences in the family environment dimensions is presented.

4

Family Environments: A Typology

In the Bullock Report entitled *A Language for Life* (1975: 286), which investigates the teaching of reading and language in English schools, it is proposed that

No child should be expected to cast off the language and culture of the home as he crosses the school threshold, nor to live and act as though school and home represent two totally separate and different cultures which have to be kept firmly apart. The curriculum should reflect many elements of that part of his life which a child lives outside school.

By examining relations between family environments and children's achievements, the purposes of the present study are in accord with the sentiments expressed in the Bullock Report. If teachers are to develop curricula that build upon differences in children's social backgrounds, then the present analysis suggests environmental dimensions that might be incorporated into the structuring of such programmes. After collecting the data for the study, I returned to the participating schools and discussed the initial findings with teachers. From those exchanges it became obvious that, for the future planning of programmes, teachers were interested in parents' responses to particular items from the interview schedule. Also, the ethclass group variations in the profiles of environment scores suggest that the adoption of one ideal-type definition of family learning environments may obscure important social-group family differences. Therefore, in the present chapter a family typology is constructed as a refinement of the ideal-type definition of an academically oriented family, developed in Chapter 2. The typology is then used to embellish the findings from Chapter 3, by examining responses to individual items from the environment schedule.

In particular, the family typology is generated from social action models devised by Merton, Parsons, Bidwell and Bernstein. For example, in an examination of relations between social structures and individuals' behaviours, Merton (1968: 186–187) constructs a typology using two elements of social and cultural structures. The first element, 'consists of culturally defined goals, purposes and interests, held out as legitimate objectives for all or for diversely located members of the society ... the prevailing goals comprise a frame of aspirational reference. They are the things "worth striving for".' Merton's second element, 'defines, regulates and controls the acceptable modes of reaching out for these goals' and it is proposed that, 'Every social group invariably couples its cultural objectives with regulations, rooted in the mores or institutions of allowable procedures for moving toward these objectives' (1968: 187). The distinction between culturally defined goals and the institutionalised means of achieving those goals is adopted as the basis for constructing the present family typology. Parents' educational and occupational aspirations for children are considered to represent a set of family goals, while the means available to assist children in achieving those objectives are defined by the other dimensions of the ideal family type, *viz.*, achievement orientations, press for English, press for dependence, individualistic-collectivistic value orientations. But the procedures adopted by parents to satisfy their aspirations may be categorised further as being either instrumental or expressive. A positive instrumental parent orientation involves, 'The capacity to do things *relatively* "well"', and incorporates the parents' responsibility to organise a supportive learning environment (Parsons, 1951: 158). In contrast, parents' expressive orientations are not related, 'to the attainment of a goal anticipated for the future, but the organization of the "flow" of gratifications (and of course the warding off of threatened deprivations)' (1951: 49). A similar dichotomy of parents' orientations is proposed by Bidwell (1972, 1973), who suggests that children's socialisation can be thought of as having two principal components: first, technical socialisation, which attempts to change children's cognitions or involves 'developing intellective and motor skills and learning items of information and systems of thought that organize them' (1972: 1); second, affective socialisation, which is related to changes in children's moral commitments or affective states. But as Bidwell (1973) warns, the distinction between technical and affective socialisation cannot be sustained empirically with much ease, for the two kinds of activities are interdependent. The constructs of instrumental and expressive orientations are adopted by Bernstein (1977: 37) for an analysis of 'family settings in terms of a family's perception of the school culture; how they regard it, see it and understand it'. He proposes that a school's instrumental order relates to those activities generating the acquisition of specific skills, while the expressive order is 'that complex of behaviour and activities in the school which is to do with conduct, character and manner' and which 'tends to bind the whole school together as a distinct moral collectivity' (1977: 38–39).

The development of the family environment typology for the present chapter adopts the concepts of culturally defined goals and the means parents use to achieve those goals. These means are classified further into instrumental and expressive orientations. As indicated earlier, aspirations are used to assess parents' goals for their children. Parents' instrumental orientations are measured by achievement orientations and press for English, which gauge parents' attempts to create a supportive cognitive environment in the home and parents' efforts to teach English skills to their children. Thus, a strong family instrumental orientation is defined by high achievement orientations and strong press for English. The expressive orientations of parents are measured by press for dependence and individualistic-collectivistic value orientations. An independent-expressive score is interpreted as reflecting an environment in which parents encourage independent action by their children. Dependent-expressive scores indicate that parents attempt to maintain the family as a collectivity, as long as possible, with the implication that families will continue to transmit certain desired images of conduct. Perhaps it needs to be stated again that classifying environment orientations as strong or weak does not mean that families are being compared in an ethical sense (p. 32). Instead, when families are classified later as being, say, committed or detached, the labelling is related to the theoretical framework presented in Chapter 1, which suggests that given the realities of the distribution of social power among ethclass groups, some families are more favourably positioned than others to transmit those aspects of cultural capital associated with children's successful academic performance.

The family typology devised for the present study is shown in Figures 4.1 and 4.2. Included in Figure 4.1 are families expressing medium to high educational and occupational aspirations for their children, while Figure 4.2 represents families exhibiting low to medium aspirations. In both figures, families are classified about two axes, labelled instrumental and expressive orientations. Each quadrant in the diagrams represents a type of family environment defined by a combination of parents' aspirations and the two orientations. It is realised, of course, that families may change their positions within the typology. Children's behaviour and school performances may result in parents changing their aspirations and activities in the home. Also, changes in parents' economic circumstances or the birth of

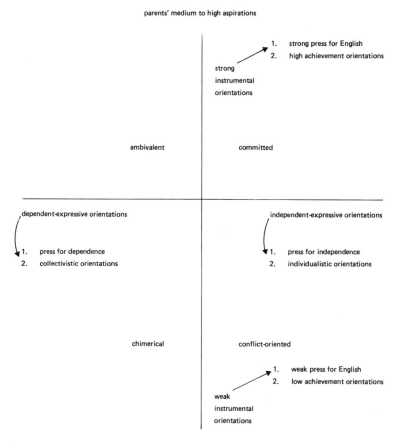

parents' medium to high aspirations

strong press for English
2. high achievement orientations

strong
instrumental
orientations

ambivalent   committed

dependent-expressive orientations   independent-expressive orientations

1. press for dependence   1. press for independence
2. collectivistic orientations   2. individualistic orientations

chimerical   conflict-oriented

1. weak press for English
2. low achievement orientations

weak
instrumental
orientations

Figure 4.1 Family typology: parents' medium to high aspirations

another child, for example, may be associated with the creation of quite different family learning environments.

In Chapter 2 it was proposed that an ideal-type definition was 'never, or only very rarely, encountered in all its purity in real life ... because it is unreal and takes us a step away from reality, it enables us to obtain a better intellectual and scientific grasp of reality, although necessarily a fragmented one' (Freund, 1968: 63). Similarly, the typology being presented here is a fragmented perspective of family environments. But it is hoped that the perspective will assist in the attempt to increase our understanding of ethclass group differences in parent-child interactions. In a number of cases the labels

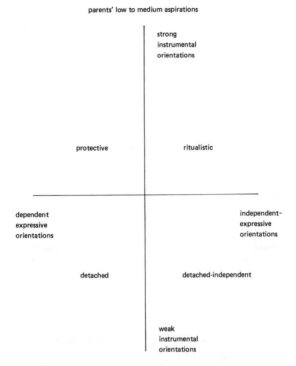

Figure 4.2   Family typology: parents' low to medium aspirations

designating the different family environments, in Figures 4.1 and 4.2, have been chosen to maintain continuity with previous models constructed by Merton and Bernstein.

In Figure 4.1, committed family environments are characterised by strong parental support for learning in the home, associated with strong press for independence. The findings in Chapter 3 suggest that environments combining such instrumental and expressive orientations are likely to be related to children's high academic achievement. Ambivalent families have parents with medium to high aspirations, who provide a supportive instrumental orientation for achievement but encourage children's dependence on the family. As Merton (1976: 8) suggests, 'the core-type of sociological ambivalence puts contradictory demands upon the occupants of a status in a particular social relation'. It is considered that the 'contradictory' orientations of parents in ambivalent families will act as a restraining force on children's performances in school. In chimerical families, parents stress dependence on the family, they have weak instrumental orientations, but they do express medium to high aspirations. While such a combination of environment dimensions is thought to be fanciful, the unreal nature of the environment may reflect parents' inability rather than their unwillingness to provide a cognitively-oriented context. Conflict-oriented environments reflect families with high aspirations, independent-expressive orientations, but weak instrumental orientations. Such an environmental category, for example, may include immigrant families who adopt expressive orientations associated with children's successful academic performance, but are unable to provide the appropriate instrumental orientation for their children.

In Figure 4.2, parents have low to medium educational and occupational aspirations for their children. The label 'ritualistic' has been adopted from Merton's typology of how people adapt their behaviour to the pressures of social structures. Merton (1968: 203–204) describes ritualism as

the abandoning or scaling down of the lofty cultural goals of great pecuniary success and rapid social mobility to the point where one's aspirations can be satisfied. But though one rejects the cultural obligation to attempt 'to get ahead in the world', though one draws in one's horizons, one continues to abide almost compulsively by institutional norms.

Ritualistic families in the present typology are those who have low to medium aspirations for children but adopt the procedures of committed families, *viz.*, strong instrumental orientations and independent-expressive orientations. Protective families are characterised by strong instrumental orientations but also by a 'protective' context for children, consisting of low to medium aspirations and a stress on children's family dependence. Families with low aspirations, weak instrumental orientations, and dependent-expressive orientations are classified as being 'detached' from mainstream social-group orientations towards education. Detached-independent families also have low to medium aspirations and weak instrumental orientations but they encourage children's independence from the family.

It is recognised that combinations of other environment variables could have been adopted to form different family typologies. While the present framework is developed from an elaboration of the ideal family type presented in Chapter 2, and is constructed to maintain continuity with some prior models, it is hoped that the typology represents an advance over what has been devised previously. In the following section of the chapter the typology is used to examine, in greater detail, ethclass group differences in family learning environments. In contrast to the previous chapter, where group differences in dimension mean scores are examined, the following analysis concentrates on responses to individual questionnaire items. Not all of the questions used to assess the elements of the typology are investigated, as such a process would become overly tedious. Instead, items are selected that are considered to be representative of the environment scales and also which aroused discussion, and often argument, when the findings were discussed with teachers.

Aspirations, instrumental and expressive orientations: ethclass group differences

From an examination of responses to questions assessing parents' aspirations and their instrumental and expressive orientations, families from the six ethclasses are located, in this section of the chapter, within the family typology. It must be emphasised, however, that the classification of ethclass families is related to the concept of a statistical average and that for each ethclass there will be families that deviate from the norm. The present analysis should be considered as providing an initial model from which researchers can proceed when investigating the learning environments of children from different social groups.

Parents' aspirations for their children

Responses to the following three items are used to examine ethclass group differences in parents' educational and occupational aspirations for their children. The numbers in parentheses following each question refer to the actual numbering of questions in part B of the family environment schedule presented in Appendix A.

1. How much education would you really like your child to receive if at all possible? (Educational aspirations, B-1.)
2. How much education do you really *expect* your child to receive? (Educational expectations, B-2.)
3. What kind of job would parents really like their children to have when they grow up, if at all possible? (Occupational aspirations, B-4.)

In relation to the first question, over 70 per cent of Greek parents and approximately 46 per cent of Southern Italian parents indicated they would like their 11-year-old child eventually to receive a university degree, if at all possible. The corresponding figures for the

Anglo-Australian middle social status and Yugoslavian families were 40 and 36 per cent, while only 30 and 24 per cent of the English and lower social status Anglo-Australian parents, respectively, expressed similar educational aspirations. At the lower levels of the educational aspiration scale, the percentage of families indicating they expected their child to either, 'leave school as soon as possible' or 'finish high school' were as follows: Anglo-Australian lower social status, 51 per cent; English, 44; Yugoslavian, 41; Anglo-Australian middle social status, 25; Southern Italian, 15; and Greek, 12 per cent. These initial findings suggest that Greek and Southern Italian families may be classified as high aspiring, the Anglo-Australian middle social-status group as having medium to high aspirations, with the remaining ethclasses located in the typology depicting low to medium aspiring families. It must be remembered, however, that the Yugoslavian findings are based on a relatively small sample of families.

The second question attempts to assess, what may be considered as more realistic educational expectations and generally the parents responded accordingly. For example, 44, 27 and 26 per cent of Greek, Southern Italian and Anglo-Australian lower social-status families, respectively, indicated that they expected their child at least to graduate from university. The corresponding percentages for the other ethclasses were: Yugoslavian, 14; English, 13; and Anglo-Australian lower social status, 10 per cent.

Percentage distributions for occupational aspirations reflect the findings of the first two questions, with 74 and 60 per cent of Greek and Southern Italian parents, respectively, indicating that they would like their child to have an occupation requiring at least graduation from high school plus some college training for occupations such as nursing or teaching. The corresponding figure was 50 per cent for Anglo-Australian middle status families, while 40, 38 and 35 per cent of Yugoslavian, Anglo-Australian lower social status and English parents, respectively, expressed similar occupational aspirations.

In Figure 4.3, the standardised mean scores for responses to the three aspiration questions, for each ethclass, are presented. Throughout the chapter, when questions include responses from both parents, a single averaged-parent score has been used in calculating profile mean values. The profiles in Figure 4.3 indicate that, in relation to the other groups in the sample, the Greek and Southern Italian families may generally be classified as belonging to the typology involving high aspirations (see Figure 4.1). Because the mean aspiration scores of the middle social-status Anglo-Australian parents are above the overall standardised mean of fifty, these families are categorised as having medium to high aspirations. The

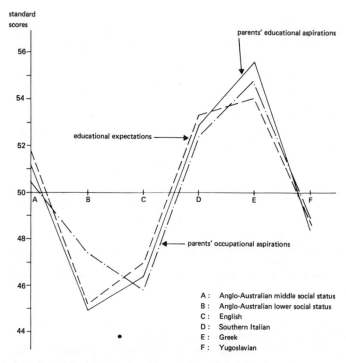

Figure 4.3 Profiles of parents' aspiration scores

typical families from the English and low social-status Anglo-Australian groups are located in the typology of low aspiring families. The classification of Yugoslavian families is less clear, but as the mean scores on the three questions fall below the standardised mean for the total sample of families, they are placed in the topology of low to medium aspiring parents.

Parents' instrumental orientations

Instrumental orientations are assessed using the environment dimensions of achievement orientations and press for English. The analyses of individual items are summarised in Figures 4.4 and 4.5. In Figure 4.4, the profiles show the ethclass group differences in mean responses to the following questions:

A. Would you know what topic your child is studying (or has just finished doing) in, say, English or arithmetic, at school? (B-35.)

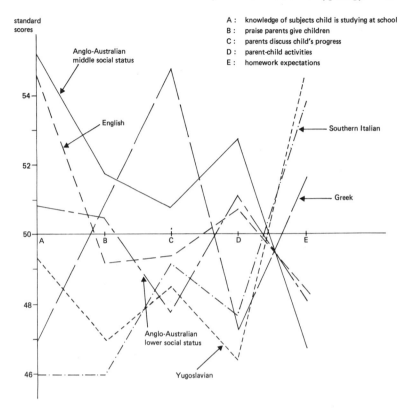

A : knowledge of subjects child is studying at school
B : praise parents give children
C : parents discuss child's progress
D : parent-child activities
E : homework expectations

Figure 4.4 Profiles of instrumental orientation scores: achievement orientations

B. If your child does well in schoolwork, how often do you praise her/him? (B-27.)
C. How often do the parents discuss their child's progress at school? (B-19.)
D. How many outside activities have the parents and child engaged in together during the past six months? (B-33.)
E. How much homework do the parents expect their child to do each week? (B-29.)

The profile scores show great variation among the ethclasses in parents' responses to the questions. For example, in relation to other ethclasses, Anglo-Australian middle social-status parents typically have detailed knowledge of the topics their 11-year-old child is

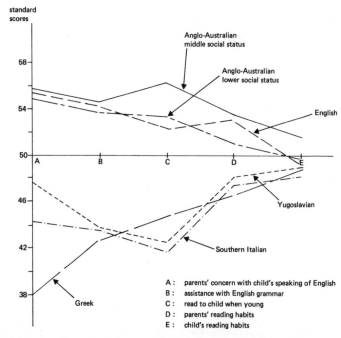

Figure 4.5 Profiles of instrumental orientations: press for English

studying at school, they regularly praise their child for work done at school, they discuss quite often the child's school progress, they are actively involved with the child in outside activities, but the parents do not expect the child to do very much homework. In contrast, Southern Italian parents have little specific knowledge of the topics their child is working on at school, they rarely praise the child for work completed at school, they have a reasonable number of discussions between themselves about the child's school progress, they are involved in few outside activities with the child, but they have high expectations of the amount of time the child should devote to homework. Greek parents express a particularly varied pattern of responses. In relation to families from the other ethclasses, they offer quite regular praise for their child's school achievements, they discuss very regularly their child's school progress, they participate in very few outside activities with the child, and they have very high expectations of the amount of time their child should be involved with homework.

The profiles in Figure 4.4 suggest that, for the present sample and for the questions analysed so far, the Anglo-Australian middle social-status families may be classified as generally expressing strong instrumental orientations for academic achievement, while Southern Italian families typically have weak instrumental orientations. Placement of the other four ethclass groups is less certain. Therefore, before attempting any further classification of families into the typology, the press for English scores are considered.

The profiles in Figure 4.5 show the ethclass group differences in parents' responses to the following questions:

A. How particular would you say you are about the way your child speaks English (good vocabulary, correct grammar)? (B-10.)

B. How often would you help your child with her/his English grammar (e.g. tell the child how to construct sentences, when to use certain words,...)? (B-23.)

C. When the child was small, before she/he started school, how often did you read to her/him, in English? (B-14.)

D. How many books, in English, would you read in a month? (B-13.)

E. How many books does the child bring home each month? (B-16.)

As must be expected, the scores reflecting parent-child interactions in English are much higher for the three Anglo groups when compared with the three non-Anglo ethclasses. When asked, for example, 'How particular would you say you are about the way your child speaks English?' the following percentages of parents indicated they were 'unable to help': Greek, 82 per cent; Southern Italian, 53 per cent; and Yugoslavian, 41 per cent, while no parents from the three Anglo groups gave such a response. Such a finding supports a claim offered earlier that a weak family instrumental orientation may indicate that parents, rather than being uninterested, are unable to provide a cognitively oriented family environment, as defined in the present study. When parents were asked, 'How often would you help your child with her/his English grammar?' the percentage of parents indicating they 'never' offered assistance were: Greek, 87 per cent; Southern Italian, 75; Yugoslavian, 68; English, 19; Anglo-Australian lower social status, 14; and Anglo-Australian middle social status, 10 per cent. The profile scores also show large group mean differences in the amount of parental reading to the child before she/he started going to school. For example, the following figures relate to the responses by parents indicating that they either read to the young child 'nearly every day (three to five times a week)' or 'just about every day'. The first percentage refers to mothers' responses while the percentage in parentheses relates to the corresponding responses of fathers: Anglo-Australian middle social status, 82 (29); Anglo-Australian lower social status, 65(19); English, 54(30); Greek, 22 (6);

Southern Italian, 18(9) and Yugoslavian 31 (13). While the group differences in the reading habits of parents and children are smaller, the findings show that generally, parents read few books in a month. When all books are considered, whether written in English or another language, the following percentages of parents indicated that in a month they typically read 'no books' or 'less than one' (again the first figure for each group is for mothers' responses, while the second percentage relates to the fathers' replies): Anglo-Australian middle social status, 30 (39); Anglo-Australian lower social status, 48 (69); English, 40 (50); Greek, 63 (71); Southern Italian, 66 (78); and Yugoslavian, 63 (67). Also, parents' perceptions of their child's reading habits, as assessed by the total number of books brought into the home by the child, suggests that many of the 11-year-olds may read few books at home. The following figures show the percentage of parents stating that their child: (a) doesn't bring home any books in a month or brings home one or two a month, and (b) brings home about one book a week. The percentages for the second alternative are placed in parentheses: Anglo-Australian middle social status, 22 (37); Anglo-Australian lower social status, 30 (41); English, 33 (40); Greek 27 (52); Southern Italian, 34 (45); and Yugoslavian 27 (50).

After considering the combination of profile scores in Figures 4.4 and 4.5, the Anglo-Australian middle social status families are classified as having strong instrumental orientations, the Anglo-Australian lower social-status and English families as having medium to strong instrumental orientations, while the three non-Anglo groups are classified as having families with weak to medium instrumental orientations.

Parents' expressive orientations

The expressive orientations of parents are assessed using the environmental dimensions of individualistic-collectivistic value orientations and press for independence. In Figure 4.6, the profiles show the ethclass group differences in (a) the press for independence score, which is calculated from ten items assessing the age that parents allow their child to engage in a set of activities independently (see p. 000), and (b) parents'responses to the following five statements.
A. Even when a boy gets married his main loyalty still belongs to his parents (B-36a).
B. Even when a girl gets married her main loyalty still belongs to her parents (B-36b).
C. When the time comes for a son to take a job, he should try and stay near his parents, even if it means giving up a good job opportunity (B-36c).

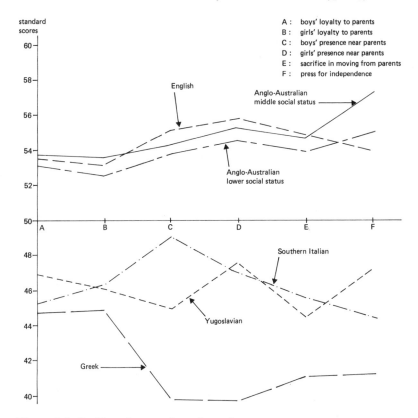

standard scores

A : boys' loyalty to parents
B : girls' loyalty to parents
C : boys' presence near parents
D : girls' presence near parents
E : sacrifice in moving from parents
F : press for independence

English

Anglo-Australian
middle social status

Anglo-Australian
lower social status

Southern Italian

Yugoslavian

Greek

Figure 4.6 Profiles of expressive orientations

D. When the time comes for a daughter to take a job, she should try and stay near her parents, even if it means giving up a good job opportunity (B-36d).

E. Nothing in life is worth the sacrifice of moving away from one's parents (B-36e).

The items have been rated such that high scores represent individualistic rather than collectivistic value orientations. In Figure 4.6, the findings reflect, in a more detailed manner, the results from Figure 3.9. In relation to the total sample of families, the three Anglo groups have independent-expressive orientations, while the three non-Anglo groups have dependent-expressive orientations. In particular, the Greek parents have very strong collectivistic-orientations. For example, in responses to the questions regarding the possibility that children should try and stay near their parents even if it meant giving up a good job opportunity, 75 and 45 per cent of Greek parents agreed with the proposition for girls and boys, respectively. The corresponding percentages for the other ethclasses were: Anglo-Australian middle social status, 4 (1); Anglo-Australian lower social status, 7 (2); English, 4 (1); Southern Italian, 29 (11); and Yugo-slavian, 27 (18).

The average ages that parents allowed, or would allow, their child to engage in certain activities are shown in Table 4.1 and they reveal again that non-Anglo-group parents generally express stronger press for dependence than do the Anglo-group families. Greek, Southern Italian and Yugoslavian parents , for example, indicate that typically they would not allow their child to go on an overnight trip organised by the school until the child reached the age of about 13, which is generally after children have completed elementary school. Similary, Greek and Southern Italian parents state they would not allow their child to go and stay at a friend's place overnight, until a much later age than that expressed by Anglo-group families. Although parents' independence-orientations constitute only one element of expressive orientations, the present results indicate that teachers who are or-ganising activities for children from different ethclasses must always be aware of and sensitive to the expressive orientations of families.If

TABLE 4.1 *Mean ages: press for independence dimension*

Independence items[a]	A	B	C	D	E	F
Earn spending money	10[b]	10	10	17	13	12
Bed-time age	6	6	7	7	7	7
Know way around neighbourhood	8	8	9	9	9	8
Visit friends' homes	8	8	8	12	10	10
Stay alone at home at night	14	15	15	15	16	14
Make own decisions	10	11	12	13	13	11
Act as babysitter	16	16	16	16	16	16
Sleep at friend's place	9	10	11	17	15	13
Go to movies alone	14	14	14	17	17	15
Go on overnight trip organised by school	9	10	9	13	13	12

A = Anglo-Australian middle status   D = Greek
B = Anglo-Australian lower status   E = Southern Italian
C = English   F = Yugoslavian
[a] Refers to question in the environment schedule, Appendix A.
[b] Mean ages rounded to nearest whole number.

such orientations are not respected, then conflicts are likely to develop between schools and families.

On an expressive-orientation scale, as assessed by independence orientations, the findings show that the three Anglo groups may be classified in the family typology as having strong independent-expressive orientations while the three non-Anglo groups may be categorised as having medium to strong dependent-expressive orientations.

The final classification of the six ethclasses, in the family typology, is summarised in Table 4.2. Anglo-Australian middle social-status families are the only group categorised as committed, which is a classification equivalent to the academically oriented family definition constructed in Chapter 2. The chimerical nature of the Greek and Southern Italian families supports the findings of Rosen (1959), who observed a similar pattern of relationships between environmental variables for families from these two groups in the United States. Yugoslavian families are perhaps the most difficult to classify as they often fall between the Anglo and other non-Anglo groups on the environment measures. They have been labelled 'chimerical-detached' because of the low to medium classification for parents' aspirations which suggested that a number of the families could have been placed in the typology of medium to high aspiring parents.

The classification of families in the typology suggests that educators who work with children from different ethclasses need to develop programmes with varied environmental goals, if children's

TABLE 4.2 *Family typology: classification of families*

Ethclass	Aspirations	Instrumental orientations	Expressive orientations	Family type
Anglo-Australian middle status	medium-high	strong	independent	committed
Anglo-Australian lower status	low	medium-strong	independent	ritualistic
English	low	medium-strong	independent	ritualistic
Greek	high	weak-medium	dependent	chimerical
Southern Italian	high	weak-medium	dependent	chimerical
Yugoslavian	low-medium	weak-medium	dependent	chimerical-detached

school achievements are to be influenced. For ritualistic families from the Anglo-Australian lower social status and English groups, for example, parents' aspirations need to be investigated, which implies examining the complex links between parents' economic circumstances, the biographies of parents including an analysis of their own realised and unfulfilled ambitions, and parents' perceptions of the associations between schooling and their children's long-term educational attainment. In chimerical families, educators need to be aware of the possible early dissatisfaction of parents with schooling if parents'aspirations for their children's achievements are not fulfilled. If the disjunction continues between the culturally prescribed aspirations and the inability or unwillingness to adopt the socially structured values for realising the aspirations, then parents may begin to lower their expectations and become 'detached' families in relation to children's school performances. As Merton (1976: 11) suggests, such a reaction is likely to occur 'when cultural values are internalized by those whose position in the social structure does not give them access to act in accord with the values they have been taught to prize'. When the present analysis of the family typology is associated with the profiles of academic performance shown in Figure 3.8, the findings suggest the proposition that, by the end of elementary school, parents in chimerical families may already be expressing less satisfaction with schooling than parents from other family types. In the following section of the chapter, parents' satisfaction with certain aspects of schooling are examined.

Parents' satisfaction with schooling

In Chapter 2 it was noted that parents' satisfaction with their child's schooling was not included as a dimension of the academically oriented family ideal-type, as previous research has produced ambiguous findings regarding associations between measures of parents' satisfactions with schooling and children's achievements. Instead, it was suggested that the following proposition would be examined: the relations between parents' satisfaction and children's academic achievement varies at different levels of children's intelligence and measures of their school-related attitudes. Also, in the previous section of the chapter it was observed that generally, children with the lowest academic performance were from ethclasses in which parents expressed the highest educational and occupational aspirations for their children. It was then proposed that because these parents were not having their aspirations fulfilled in relation to children's achievement, they may be less satisfied with schooling than are other parents. These sets of propositions are examined in this section of the chapter.

Parents' satisfaction with schooling: ethclass group differences

Parents' satisfaction with schooling was assessed using twenty items from the family environment schedule (see pp. 141–144). After factoring the responses to the items, three satisfaction factors were identified and labelled: parents' satisfaction with teachers, parents' satisfaction with teaching, and parents' satisfaction with school. The satisfaction with teachers scale consists of items such as, in the school my child attends: teachers seem to treat all children very fairly, teachers are very friendly and approachable, teachers seem to be very interested in my child's education, and teachers give the impression they want to keep parents out of the school. Parents' satisfaction with teaching was measured by asking parents to rate how they perceived the quality of teaching, in their child's school, of: mathematics, reading, English, sports, social studies, art and music. Items used to gauge parents' satisfaction with their child's school included, How satisfied would you say you are with the school that your child attends?, and, in the school my child attends: there is not enough homework, there is not enough discipline, too much time is spent on subjects such as art, music and drama, the methods of teaching seem to be too progressive, and not enough time is spent on teaching the basic subjects such as reading and arithmetic.

In Figure 4.7, the profiles show the ethclass group differences in the mean scores on the three satisfaction scales. Group differences on the scale assessing satisfaction with teachers are not significant. Differences on the other two scales are small but significant and they indicate that the three non-Anglo-groups express lower satisfactions than do the parents from Anglo-group families. When the ethclass group membership data are considered as a set of mutually exclusive categories, in a multiple regression model, they are associated with 4.5 per cent of the variance in satisfaction with school scores and 6.3 per cent of the variance in satisfaction with teaching. These initial findings provide tentative support for the proposition that chimerical families show less satisfaction with schooling than do other family types.

In Table 4.3, the percentage of parents responding to those questions used to measure satisfaction with teaching and satisfaction with school are shown. Responses are categorised into three groups, indicating parents who 'agree or agree strongly', 'disagree or disagree

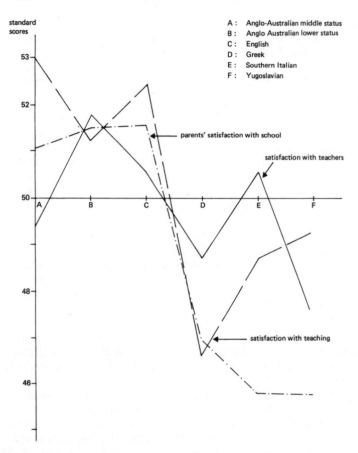

Figure 4.7   Profiles of parents' satisfaction with school scores

strongly' and those indicating they 'don't know'. Typically the figures reveal that parents express general satisfaction with teachers. For example, over 90 per cent of parents 'agree' or 'agree strongly' that 'teachers are very friendly and approachable', approximately 80 per cent from each ethclass agree that, 'teachers seem to treat all children very fairly', and over 80 per cent disagree with the statement that, 'teachers give the impression they want to keep parents out of the school'. The most significant differences occur in the item related to homework, with the non-Anglo group expressing greater dissatisfaction than the Anglo groups, with the amount of homework set by schools. An important statistic, especially for the non-Anglo groups, relates to the percentage of parents who offer a 'don't know' response to questions. If the 'don't know' statistic is associated with replies to the item asking, whether parents receive enough information about how their child is performing in school, then the magnitude of the problem confronting schools in trying to develop school-family relationships is dramatically emphasised.

In Table 4.4, the percentage responses to items assessing parents' satisfaction with teaching are presented. Responses are classified into three categories, indicating that parents perceived the teaching of a particular subject in their child's school as being: 'good or very good', 'poor or very poor', 'don't know'. Generally, the Anglo groups indicate satisfaction with the quality of teaching with some reservations about art and music, sport, and English. The large percentage of Greek and Yugoslavian parents who state they 'don't know' how satisfactory the teaching is of English and reading, relates to the earlier finding that many parents from these two ethclasses were 'unable' to help their children with the teaching of English. Southern Italian parents, however, who also indicated an inability to assist their children with English express much satisfaction with the teaching of English and reading in their child's school.

In general, the percentage figures from Tables 4.3 and 4.4 provide further support for the proposition that Anglo-group parents express greater satisfaction with their child's schooling than do parents from non-Anglo social groups. Perhaps the major implication of the analysis is that parents need much more information about their child's schooling before they are able to make critical judgements. The fact that so many parents were willing to admit they 'don't know' about their child's schooling, provides some form of support for the validity of parents' responses to the interview schedule.

Parents' satisfaction, children's intelligence and academic achievement

An examination of zero-order correlations indicated that while the measures of academic achievement were not associated with parents' satisfaction with teachers, they did have low but significant associations with parents' satisfaction with teaching and school. In the total sample, for example, satisfaction with school has correlations of 0.13, 0.20 and 0.23 with mathematics, word knowledge and word comprehension, respectively, while the corresponding relations between satisfaction with teaching and achievement are 0.09, 0.21 and 0.20.

Regression surface analysis was used to investigate the relations between the satisfaction scores and children's achievement, at dif-

TABLE 4.3 *Parents' satisfaction with schools and teachers: percentage responses*

Questionnaire item[a]		Anglo-Australian middle status	Anglo-Australian lower status	English	Greek	Southern Italian	Yugoslavian
Not enough homework	A[b,c]	35	37	36	77	66	54
	DA	63	60	61	19	28	32
	DK	1	3	3	4	6	14
Not enough discipline	A	39	44	41	32	36	45
	DA	53	52	58	39	52	36
	DK	8	4	1	29	12	18
Too much time on art, music, drama	A	17	18	11	20	13	18
	DA	75	69	77	26	50	50
	DK	8	13	11	54	37	32
Not enough time on reading, arithmetic	A	40	50	48	31	34	46
	DA	55	54	48	27	33	27
	DK	5	5	4	41	33	27
Methods of teaching too progressive	A	31	35	26	22	23	27
	DA	62	55	65	16	41	36
	DK	7	9	9	62	36	36
Don't receive enough information from school	A	27	27	21	36	21	40
	DA	72	72	79	61	78	55
	DK	1	1	—	3	1	5
Teachers very friendly	A	95	97	97	96	90	91
	DA	4	2	3	—	3	—
	DK	1	1	—	3	7	9
Teachers treat children fairly	A	79	88	82	78	82	77
	DA	14	5	12	4	4	5
	DK	7	7	6	18	14	18
Teachers interested in child's education	A	89	87	94	79	86	68
	DA	7	7	4	8	4	—
	DK	4	6	1	13	10	32

	Anglo-Australian middle status	Anglo-Australian lower status	English	Greek	Southern Italian	Yugoslavia
Teachers want to keep parents out of school A	8	4	75	6	8	5
DA	91	94	5	92	91	90
DK	1	2	20	2	1	5

a Relates to question in family environment schedule, Appendix A.
b A indicates that parents 'agree or agree strongly' with the questionnaire item, DA indicates parents 'disagree or disagree strongly', while DK represents 'don't know' responses.
c The first six items assess parents' satisfaction with school while the following four items assess parents' satisfaction with teachers.

TABLE 4.4 *Parents' satisfaction with teaching: percentage responses*

Subject		Anglo-Australian middle status	Anglo-Australian lower status	English	Greek	Southern Italian	Yugoslavia
Mathematics	G[a]	80	83	8	44	55	55
	P	13	9	10	22	16	22
	DK	7	8	9	34	29	23
Reading	G	78	82	87	53	82	59
	P	15	13	10	7	11	9
	DK	7	5	3	40	7	32
English	G	68	73	74	54	82	55
	P	25	19	19	3	6	22
	DK	7	8	7	43	12	23
Sports	G	59	67	61	65	76	68
	P	30	23	23	2	8	5
	DK	11	10	16	33	16	27
Social studies	G	77	78	84	47	58	54
	P	12	7	7	4	12	5
	DK	11	15	9	49	30	41
Art/Music	G	60	60	59	50	37	27
	P	20	15	18	5	34	18
	DK	20	25	23	45	29	55

a G indicates that parents rate the teaching of the subject as good or very good, P indicates a poor or very poor rating, while DK represents 'don't know' responses.

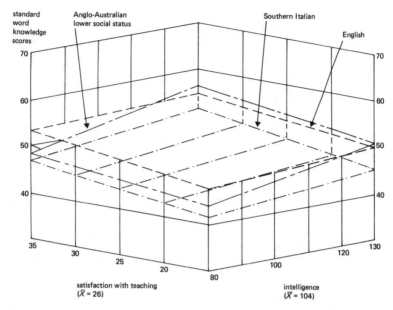

Figure 4.8   Fitted-word knowledge scores in relation to intelligence and parents' satisfaction with teaching. Mean scores relate to the total sample of children.

ferent levels of intelligence. Again, the surfaces were plotted from regression models of the form:

$$Z = aX + bY + cXY + dX^2 + eY^2 + \text{constant}$$

where Z, X, and Y represent measures of academic achievement, intelligence, and parents' satisfactions, respectively. In the space available it is not possible to present all the regression surfaces generated from the data. Therefore, three surfaces have been plotted on one figure as they reflect many of the findings from the other regression equations, especially those involving the word-test scores. In Figure 4.8, the surfaces show the regression-fitted relations between parents' satisfaction with teaching and word knowledge scores at different levels of intelligence. The shapes of the surfaces reveal that the curvilinear and interaction terms were not significant in the regression models, after adjusting significance levels for the design effects of the samples. At each level of intelligence, large increments in parents' satisfaction with teaching are associated with small increments in children's word knowledge scores. As the satisfaction scores increase, for example, from a low of fifteen to a high of thirty-five, the regression-estimated word knowledge scores for Southern Italian, Anglo-Australian lower social status, and English children increase by approximately seven, six and five points, respectively, at each level of intelligence. Also, at each level of parents' satisfaction, increments in children's intelligence are related to small increases in the word knowledge scores. Similar surfaces are generated when satisfaction with school scores are used in the regression equations. Also, the shapes of the surfaces for word comprehension are, in general, similar to those shown in Figure 4.8. For mathematics, however, increments in satisfaction scores are not related to changes in achievement at different levels of intelligence. Therefore, the findings of the analysis provide only weak support for the proposition that, at different levels of intelligence, increments in parents' satisfaction with schooling are related to increases in children's academic achievement.

Parents' satisfaction, attitudes to school and children's achievement

Regression surface analysis indicated that within each ethclass there were few significant relationships between parents' satisfaction and academic achievement at different levels of children's affective commitment to school and academic adjustment to school. Generally, the analyses provide support for previous research that has observed weak relations between parents' satisfaction and children's achievement. In Chapter 3 it was suggested, however, that some of the dimensions of the academically oriented family-type may act as threshold variables, such that until certain levels of these particular dimensions are attained, other environment variables will have limited associations with children's cognitive performance. In particular, it was suggested that low press for English may, in a sense, encircle a child, preventing other environment variables from substantially interacting with the child to influence academic achievement (see p. 62). Such a proposition is tested in the final section of the chapter, in which relations between parents' satisfactions and academic achievement are examined at different levels of press for English.

Parents' satisfaction, press for English and children's achievement

In Figure 4.9, the regression surfaces show the regression-fitted relations between parents' satisfaction with school and word comprehension, at different levels of press for English. The shapes of the surfaces for the Greek and Southern Italian children provide tentative support for the proposition that press for English may act as a threshold variable. In the regression models for the two non-Anglo

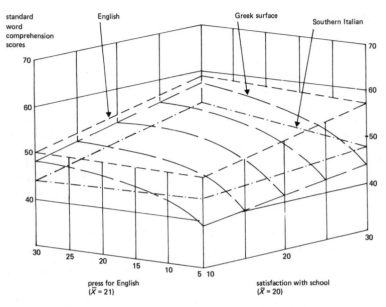

Figure 4.9 Fitted-word comprehension scores in relation to parents'
satisfaction with school and press for English. Mean scores
relate to the total sample of children.

groups the interaction term is significant. At a press for English score
of five, for example, the regression-fitted word comprehension values
for Greek children are thirty-nine and forty-three, at parents' satisfaction scores of ten and thirty, respectively. The corresponding
fitted-word scores, at a press for English value of thirty, are forty-
eight and fifty-eight. For Southern Italian children the corresponding
comprehension scores at a low press for English value of five are
forty-five and forty-seven, while at a press for English value of thirty,
the comprehension scores are forty-four and fifty-three. In the English
group, at each level of press for English, increases in satisfaction
scores from ten to thirty are associated with increments of eight
points in comprehension scores.

At each satisfaction level, increments in press for English scores are
related to sizeable increases in Greek children's comprehension
scores, but are not associated with changes in the performances of
the English children. Similar sets of relations are present for word
knowledge scores, while the associations between parents' satisfactions and mathematics performance at different values of press
for English are not significant.

Again the analysis suggests that parents' satisfactions with schooling have weak predictive validities in relation to children's achievements. In part, the low associations reflect the limited variabllity in the satisfaction scores within ethclasses. Also, the findings suggest that many parents, by responding in the form of 'don't know', are unsure about their child's school learning environment and therefore the present data provide only a very approximate measure of satisfactions. While there is some support for the proposition that parents of chimerical-type families express less satisfaction with schooling than do other parents, the results also indicate a large amount of expressed parental satisfaction. But because of the restrictions of the satisfaction measure, it is perhaps worth stating Acland's (1975: 9) concerns about parents' satisfactions so that we, as educators, do not become overly complacent with findings such as those presented here. Acland propses that, 'The way people articulate ideas about schools and their habits of thought about education are going to be shaped, and limited, by the contemporary organization of schools'. He suggests that

> At the moment, schools are run like monopolies, parents do not have extensive or effective involvement, and they appear to be broadly accepting of what goes on in schools ... So long as schools manage the business of education without drawing attention to themselves, parents will endorse their efforts. But this endorsement is not necessarily the result of a careful appraisal of the merits of schools, and it would be rash to conclude on the basis of simple survey evidence that schools are giving parents what they want.

These strong sentiments expressed by Acland indicate the need for more sensitive research of parents' satisfactions. Future studies of parent-teacher relations might usefully adopt Merton's (1976: 25) distinction between the interpersonal and social-structural elements of such relations. Merton suggests that in any social relation, 'The degree of satisfaction is only the interpersonal element', while the normative structure of the relation provides the element of social structure.

The present chapter shows that for an enriched understanding of children's family learning environments it has been useful to develop a typology based on the constructs of parents' aspirations, instrumental and expressive orientations. In the following chapter these constructs are used again to examine an interactionism framework involving family environments, individual characteristics, and children's academic achievement.

5

Families, Individual Characteristics and Children's Academic Achievement

In educational research of children's behaviour, investigators have tended to adopt either a situationism model where behaviour is related to measures of social contexts, or a trait framework in which behaviour is associated with children's individual characteristics. It is an assumption of the present research, however, that behaviour is related to a continuous interaction between person characteristics and social situations (see p. 26). Cronbach and Snow (1977) indicate, for example, the desirability of examining interactions between children's individual characteristics and the teaching situations they encounter, when attempting to explain variations in children's school performances. They have shown that children bring to learning situations (treatments) a variety of characteristics (aptitudes) that influence their responses to the learning contexts, with the result that treatments are often not equally effective along the entire range of aptitudes. Also, in studies of social environments such as classrooms, university residences, psychiatric wards, university departments and alcoholism treatment centres, Moos (1974, 1975, 1979) has observed that individuals' adaptations to different social contexts are related to a variety of person characteristics. In the construction of a conceptual framework for analysing the ecology of human development, Bronfenbrenner (1977) proposes that interactions between person variables and environments should be considered as a system with very specific properties. He states that, '*The ecology of human development is the scientific study of the progressive, mutual accommodation, throughout the life span, between a growing human organism and the changing immediate environments in which it lives*' (1977: 514). It is then suggested that

> *If you wish to understand the relation between the developing person and some aspect of his or her environment, try to budge the one, and see what happens to the other.* Implicit in this injunction is the recognition that the relation between person and the environment

has the properties of a system with a momentum of its own; the only way to discover the nature of this inertia and its interdependencies is to try and disturb the existing balance. (1977: 518.)

In the present chapter, regression surface analysis is used to examine an interactionism model, involving relations between academic achievement and measures of individual characteristics (intelligence, school-related attitudes) at different levels of family environment dimensions, for children from the different ethclasses.

Before considering the interactionism model, however, regression planes are constructed to examine propositions suggested by the analyses presented in earlier chapters. Within the ethclasses, relations are examined between academic performance and combinations of components of the family typology developed in the previous chapter, and also between achievement and measures of both intelligence and school-related attitudes.

Academic achievement and family environment: ethclass group differences

Findings from previous chapters have revealed ethclass group differences in the learning environments that parents create for their children, and have shown that the learning contexts are associated with ethclass group variations in children's cognitive performance. The results have not indicated, however, how children's academic achievement might be related to the interaction of different environment dimensions in each ethclass. Except for the investigation of parents' satisfaction with schooling, the study, so far, has not examined the proposition suggested in Chapter 3 that 'some of the dimensions of the family typology might act as threshold variables, such that until certain levels of those particular dimensions are attained other environment dimensions might have limited associations with children's performances.'In particular, it was proposed that for non-Anglo-group children who are taught in English-speaking classrooms, family dimensions like low press for English might act as rigid boundaries restricting relations between academic performance and other environmental influences such as parents' aspirations. Associations are examined, in the present section of the chapter, between academic achievement and the components of the family typology, *viz.*, parents' aspirations, instrumental orientations and expressive orientations. Regression surfaces are plotted, for different ethclasses, to investigate relations implied by the following three research models:

1. *f*(aspirations, press for English) → word knowledge
2. *f*(aspirations, value orientations) → word comprehension
3. *f*(press for English, value orientations) → word knowledge

These models are chosen as they generate surfaces that reflect the nature of many of the relationships among the variables in the study and also show the diversity of these relationships between the ethclasses. By examining the three models within ethclasses, the analysis is an attempt to provide support for Batten's (1975: 27) contention that 'we cannot justify the separation of environmental variables into "attitude" and "circumstance" groupings as though attitudes are formed in the minds of individuals without reference to their circumstances'. Batten is extremely critical of research attempting to show that home attitudinal variables have greater impact on children's educational attainment than do measures of material and socio-economic circumstances (also see Bernstein and Davies, 1969; Connell, 1972, 1974; and Halsey, 1975). For example, Batten (1975: 31) goes on to suggest

> that if literacy variables become interpreted as circumstances, then they may be regarded as somehow being more the consequence of social influences and more potentially amenable to social action. If, on the other hand, literacy variables are seen as attitudes, they may be seen as representing in those with poor attitudes (i.e. low scores) recalcitrance, indifference and sometimes even inability.

Similarly, Bernstein (1977: 27) states that, 'Class acts crucially on all agencies of cultural reproduction and therefore on *both* the family and the school.' He suggests

> I know of no class society which *deliberately* and *rationally* attempts to ensure that all social groups can participate equally in the creation, production and distribution of what are considered as value, goods and services. ... it must necessarily follow that lower working-class children are today crucially disadvantaged. ... Class is a fundamental category of exclusion and this is reproduced in various ways in schools, through the social context and forms of transmission of education. (1977: 27–28.)

The dependence of family environment variables on family social circumstances is meant to be reflected in the regression surface analyses. It should be noted that in the following investigations, Yugoslavian families are deleted from the study. The relatively small sample of these families would have permitted an accumulation of chance statistical errors to affect the results from the regression models. Also, in each regression surface the scores have been con-

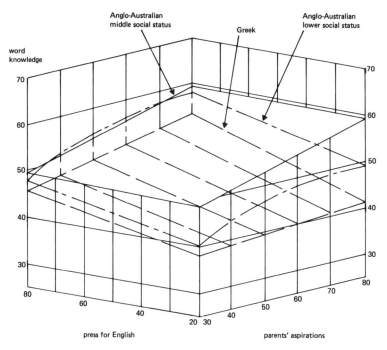

Figure 5.1 Fitted-word knowledge scores in relation to parents' aspirations and press for English

verted to standard values with means of fifty and standard deviations of ten.

f*(parents' aspirations, press for English)* → *word knowledge*

In Figure 5.1, the surfaces show the regression-fitted relations between parents' educational and occupational aspirations and children's word knowledge scores at different levels of press for English. The shapes of the three planes indicate the possible diversity of relations that may be present between the same set of variables, for families from different ethclasses. Such diversity provides support for Frideres (1977: 145) claim that research of family socialisation processes has been extremely restricted as 'Few studies have provided comparative data on a variety of family issues using ethnicity as an independent (or intervening) variable.' Similarly, Havighurst (1976) observes that if our understanding of differences in children's cognitive development is to be enriched, then it will be necessary to compare data from different social status and ethnic groups.

For Anglo-Australian middle social-status children, the shape of the regression surface reveals that at each press for English level, increases in parents' aspirations are related to increments in word knowledge scores. For example, at each press for English level, as the aspiration values change from a low of thirty to a high of eighty, the regression-fitted word knowledge scores increase by approximately ten points. At each level of parents' aspirations, however, changes in the press for English values are not associated with variation in the word knowledge values. Thus, for Anglo-Australian middle social-status families, the proposition suggesting that low press for English may restrict relations between academic performance and other environment dimensions, is not supported. The surface for the Greek children reflects regression models in which criterion measures have significant linear associations with the two environment dimensions and are related also to the interaction between the environment measures. At a low press for English value of twenty, for example, the increase in Greek children's word knowledge scores is not significant as the parents' aspiration scores increase from thirty to eighty. The corresponding increase in word scores, at the highest press for English value, is approximately eight points. That is, the shape of the Greek surface suggests that low press for English scores may be obscuring potential associations between parents' aspirations and children's school performance. Also, the significant relation between the achievement scores and the product of the environment dimensions shows that increments in press for English are associated with greater increases in word values at higher, rather than at lower, parents' aspiration scores. Only when the press for English scores are high does the Greek surface begin to approach the level of the regression plane of the middle social-status children. For Anglo-Australian lower social-status children, increases in the environment dimension scores, in relation to each other, are associated with quite sizeable increments in word knowledge performance.

The surfaces in Figure 5.1 show that for Anglo-Australian lower social-status children and, in particular, for Greek children, very high parental aspirations when associated with low press for English scores are related to low academic performance. It was proposed in the previous chapter that families with such a combination of characteristics may eventually become 'detached' from the mainstream culture's concern for education. As Bynner (1975: 14) observes, 'The failure of so many working-class parents to achieve their ambitions for their children probably lays the foundations for the alienation from the educational system which many of them clearly feel.' The present findings suggest that for investigations of parents' and children's alienation from the educational system, family environments might be divided into a set of categories such as high aspirations-low press for English and low aspirations-high press for English. Then the alienation from the school system of those parents and children belonging to the designated categories, could be compared. Bronfenbrenner (1977: 518) states that future research of ecological environments and human development might adopt such a procedure. He proposes that

> human environments and—even more so—the capacities of human beings to adapt and restructure these environments are so complex in their basic organization that they are not likely to be captured, let alone comprehended, through simplistic unidimensional research models that make no provision for assessing ecological structure and variation. Accordingly ... in ecological research the investigator seeks to 'control in' as many theoretically relevant ecological contrasts as possible. ...

As an example of his approach, Bronfenbrenner suggests that

> in studying socialization strategies, one might do well to stratify the sample not only, as is commonly done, by social class, but also by family structure. ... Such stratification in terms of two or more ecological dimensions serves the scientifically useful function of providing a systematically differentiated and thereby potentially sensitive grid that makes possible the detection and description of patterns of organism-environment interactions across a range of ecological contexts.

In relation to the surfaces in Figure 5.1, the results reveal that both press for English (an instrumental orientation) and parents' aspirations operate differentially between ethclasses in their associations with the word knowledge scores. Relations between parents' aspirations and children's achievement, at different levels of expressive orientations, are examined in the following part of the chapter.

f*(aspirations, value orientations)* → *word comprehension*

The surfaces in Figure 5.2 show the regression-fitted relations between parents' aspirations and children's word comprehension scores at different levels of individualistic-collectivistic value orientations. At each level of value orientations, large increases in parents' aspirations are associated with moderate to large increments in the word

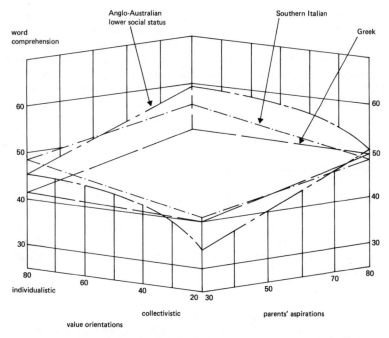

Figure 5.2   Fitted-word comprehension scores in relation to parents' aspirations and value orientations

comprehension scores, for children from each ethclass. Changes in the orientation scores from collectivistic to individualistic are related to increments in the comprehension values for the Southern Italian and Anglo-Australian lower social-status children, at each level of parents' aspirations. For Greek families, changes in value orientations are not associated with variation in the word comprehension scores. For example, at a very high aspiration level of eighty, the regression-fitted word comprehension values for Southern Italian and Greek families are forty-eight and forty-nine, respectively, at a collectivistic value orientation score of twenty. When the orientation score changes to an individualistic value of eighty, the corresponding word-test scores at the high aspiration level are fifty-five for the Southern Italians and forty-nine for the Greek children.

Once again, the regression planes in Figures 5.1 and 5.2 show that for the lower social-status 11-year-old children in the study, when high parental aspirations are associated with dependent-expressive orientations or weak instrumental orientations, they are related to low academic performance (also see Chapter 3). In a re-analysis of data from the Plowden survey of English school children (Plowden Report, 1967) and from an examination of data collected from many of the same children and parents, four years later, Bynner (1975) comes to a conclusion that is highly pertinent to the results of the present study. Bynner (1975: 10) observed that

> the most immediate effect of the failure of working-class parents to achieve their ambitions for their children when they were at primary school is a dampening of aspirations at the secondary stage. This is evident from the attitudes they express towards the age at which their child will leave school.

From his analysis, Bynner reveals that when the children were at elementary school, 'most working-class parents in the study shared the aim of middle-class parents in wanting their children to stay on at school beyond the minimum age. At secondary school the gap between the two classes widens dramatically.' His data indicate that in secondary school, 'Although the same proportion of middle-class parents want their child to stay on at school, among the working-class parents there is a marked decline' (1975: 11). That is, as suggested earlier (p. 000), if the high aspirations of lower social-status parents are not associated with children's successful achievement, then families are likely to change from being of the chimerical-type to families adopting the characteristics of the detached-types. Such a proposition has an analogy with a theoretical framework developed by Presthus (1962) to examine how individuals accommodate to large organisations. He proposes that there are upwardly mobile individuals who identify strongly with organisations and who derive great strength from their involvement with the institutions. Families in the present study who belong to the typology depicting high aspiring parents (see Figure 4.1) may be considered as perceiving themselves as 'upwardly mobile families'. Presthus claims, however, that by far the largest number of persons in organisations may be classified as indifferents. This latter classification includes individuals who possibly came to the organisation with great expectations of success and who were determined to gain satisfaction from their involvement. But because of organisational pressures these individuals lower their expectations, become alienated from the organisation, withdraw from meaningful participation in the organisation, and redirect their activities towards off-the-job activities. Such a pattern of processes is predictable for lower social-status parents, in the present study, in relation to the school system. If social and educational programmes are not developed to reduce the existing ethclass group differences in children's school performances, then it is likely that during the early years of secondary school, parents from the lower social-status groups will begin to lower their educational and occupational aspirations for their children, become increasingly alienated from the school system, withdraw support for their children at school, and adopt the expectation that their children should leave school as soon as possible. If parents' aspirations do begin to decline, then the task confronting educators in reducing ethclass group differences in achievement will become increasingly difficult, even if other aspects of the family learning environment are made more supportive. The surfaces in Figures 5.1 and 5.2 show, for example, that at reduced aspiration levels strong press for English and individualistic value orientations are generally associated with lower academic performance than when the aspiration levels are high.

In Chapter 4 the family typology that was presented was constructed about the two axes representing instrumental and expressive orientations. In the following part of this chapter, relations between achievement and measures of instrumental and expressive orientations are examined.

f *(press for English, value orientations)* → *word comprehension*

The regression-fitted relations in Figure 5.3 are between individualistic-collectivistic value orientations and word comprehension scores at different levels of press for English. For the Greek children, at each press for English level, changes in value orientations are not associated with variation in the comprehension scores; while at each level of individualistic-collectivistic orientations, increments in press for English are associated with quite sizeable changes in word-test scores. The opposite set of relations are present for the Anglo-Australian lower social-status children. At each press for English level, changes in value orientations from collectivistic to individualistic are associated with quite large increases in performance scores, while at each value orientation level, variations in press for English are related to small changes in academic achievement. The possible complexity of relations between environment dimensions and children's academic achievement is reflected in the curvature of the Southern Italian regression surface in which word comprehension scores have significant linear associations with press for English, negative curvilinear relations to the value orientations, and significant associations with the interaction between the two environment dimensions. For example at a press for English value of twenty, the regression-fitted word comprehension values for the

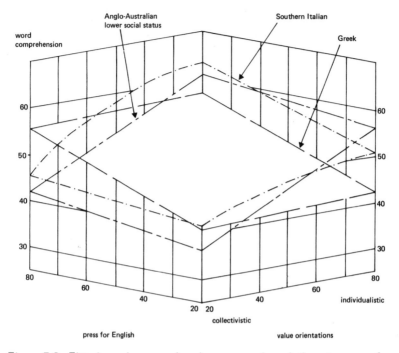

Figure 5.3 Fitted-word comprehension scores in relation to press for English and value orientations

Southern Italian children are approximately forty-two and fifty-one at value orientations of thirty and eighty, respectively. At a press for English score of eighty, however, the corresponding word-test scores are forty-five and sixty-four. In part, these findings are an artefact of the model as few Southern Italians expressed such high press for English or individualistic value orientations. But the regression planes do, quite forcibly, indicate the variable nature of relations between academic achievement and measures of instrumental and expressive orientations, for children from different ethclasses.

The regression surfaces presented in this first section of the chapter show the intricate nature of associations between ethclass group membership, family learning environments, and children's academic performance. Also, they indicate the difficulties in attempting to construct general propositions that might be applicable for relationships between variables across a number of ethclasses. The planes reveal, for example, that it is too simple a proposition to suggest that environment variables might act in the form of a hierarchy in relation to children's performances. Instead, the findings suggest that environment dimensions within each group tend to operate as a system with properties particular to each ethclass, and that to understand the mechanisms of relations between families and children's outcomes it is necessary to examine each ethclass independently, rather than construct general propositions.

At the beginning of the chapter it was proposed that variation in individuals' behaviour is most appropriately explained by a model involving both individual and environment variables. The present section of the chapter has shown that our understanding of interactionism models will be enriched by a close analysis of the environmental components of the models. In the following section of the chapter a detailed analysis is presented of the individual characteristics that will form part of the eventual interactionism framework.

Academic achievement and individual characteristics: ethclass group differences

In Chapter 3 it was suggested that the equivocal nature of the findings from previous research investigating associations between children's school-attitudes and their academic performance was, in part, related to the failure of the research to include measures of social environments (see p. 57). The inconsistent nature of the findings, however, is possibly related also to the failure of studies to include an examination of the intellectual ability of children. In a review of research, for example, Aiken (1970: 562) suggests that it may be discovered that correlations between attitudes and achievement vary with levels of ability and he proposes, 'that in the middle range of scores ... ability scores rather than attitude scores will be more accurate predictors or determiners of achievement'. Also, in a review of studies examining relations between ethnicity and mental ability scores, Gordon (1976: 167) asserts that research 'seems to have neglected the noncognitive factors in learning' and that analyses 'fail to study the compensatory role of motivation' (1976: 171). In an attempt to overcome these further restrictions of attitude-achievement research, relations between school-related attitudes and academic achievement at varying levels of children's intellectual ability, for children from different ethclasses, are examined (also see Marjoribanks 1976c, 1978c). In particular, regression surfaces are used to investigate the following three models:

1. f(intelligence, affective commitment to school) → word comprehension
2. f(intelligence, academic adjustment to school) → mathematics achievement
3. f(intelligence, academic adjustment to school) → word knowledge

Again, the particular surfaces that are plotted in the following three figures are chosen as they reflect the main differences that are present in the relations among the variables.

f(intelligence, affective commitment to school) → word comprehension

In Figure 5.4, the surfaces show the regression-fitted relations between affective commitment to school scores and word comprehension at different levels of intelligence. The shape of the regression plane for the Anglo-Australian lower social-status children reflects the majority of surfaces involving the affective commitment scores, in which the criterion achievement measures have significant linear associations with the intelligence test scores only. For Southern Italian children the regression plane shows a curvilinear relation

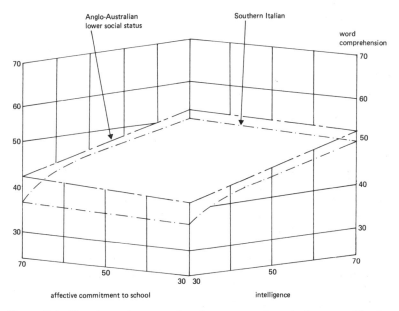

Figure 5.4 Fitted-word comprehension scores in relation to affective commitment to school and intelligence

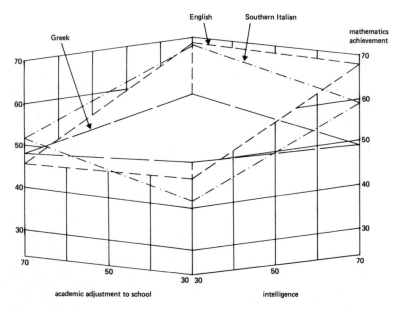

Figure 5.5 Fitted-mathematics scores in relation to academic adjustment to school and intelligence

between intelligence and word comprehension at each attitude level, with the largest increases in comprehension scores being related to changes in intelligence within the lower ability range of scores.

f*(intelligence, academic adjustment to school)* → *mathematics achievement*

The regression-fitted relations in Figure 5.5 show how academic adjustment to school is associated with mathematics achievement at different levels of intelligence. For the English children, the shape of the surface represents regression models in which academic achievement measures have significant linear associations with intelligence at different adjustment to school values, but where the criterion measures are not related to the adjustment scores at different intelligence levels. The regression plane for Southern Italian children reflects equations where criterion measures have significant linear associations with both the intelligence and adjustment to school measures. At each level of intelligence, increments in academic adjustment to school values are related to increases in mathematics performance. For example, as the adjustment scores increase from a low of

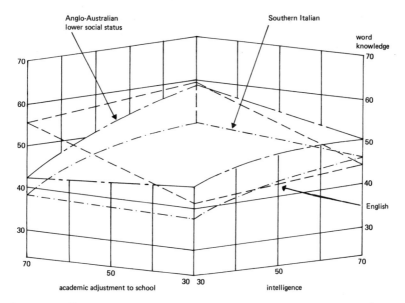

Figure 5.6 Fitted-word knowledge scores in relation to academic adjustment to school and intelligence

thirty to a high of seventy, the regression-fitted mathematics scores increase by approximately nine points, at each level of intelligence. Also, at each adjustment to school level, increments in intelligence test scores are associated with increases in mathematics performance. As ability scores increase between standard values of thirty and seventy, the regression-fitted mathematics values increase by approximately eighteen points at each attitude level. The shape of the Greek surface reflects a significant relation between mathematics and the interaction between the adjustment to school and intelligence scores. Generally, these results fail to provide support for Aiken's (1970) proposition that the relations between attitudes and achievement vary at different ability levels.

f(intelligence, academic adjustment to school) → word knowledge

In Figure 5.6, the sufaces show the relations between academic adjustment to school and word knowledge at different intelligence levels. For the English children, at each level of intelligence, increases in adjustment scores are associated with sizeable increments in word knowledge values. Increases in Southern Italian children's attitude scores are not related to changes in achievement scores, while for the Anglo-Australian lower social-status children, only at high intelligence levels are increments in attitude scores associated with increases in word knowledge performance. The differences in the shapes of these three surfaces provide support for the contention that ethclass group membership is a necessary variable to be included in analyses of human social and cognitive development.

By using regression models that include linear, interaction and curvilinear terms to generate regression surfaces for children from different ethclasses and by including a measure of intelligence in the investigation, the present analysis goes beyond much previous research that has examined associations between school-related attitudes and academic achievement. Generally, the findings suggest that: (a) at each level of intelligence, increases in the affective component of school attitudes are not associated with variations in academic achievement, (b) at each level of the affective component of school attitudes, increases in intelligence test scores are related to increments in academic achievement scores, and (c) relations between academic achievement, intelligence, and the cognitive-behavioural component of school attitudes vary widely for children from different ethclasses. Thus the findings appear to support only in part the contention by Levin (1976) that educational programmes that focus on attitudes may be able to compensate for 'disadvantages' in children's backgrounds. The present analysis suggests that changes in cognitive-behavioural aspects of children's school attitudes may be related to changes in the academic performance of children from certain low social-status ethclass groups. Educational programmes that focus on affective components of school attitudes may find it more difficult, however, to show positive relationships between attitudes and children's achievements. It is likely that the influence of changing the affective component of school attitudes on children's achievements will be transmitted through changes in a set of intervening variables such as perceptions of classroom environments, achievement motivation, self concept, and the cognitive-behavioural components of attitudes.

As indicated in Chapter 1, the present study is limited to an examination of only a few of the variables that are associated with children's achievements. Future research investigating relations between attitudes and achievement should include a set of other individual characteristics and also measures of family, neighbourhood and classroom learning environments. The present results suggest that associations between such variables should be investigated within different ethclasses for a more complete understanding of the correlates of children's academic performance. In the following section of the chapter, relations are examined between academic performance and measures of individual characteristics and family environment dimensions considered together in the same regression models.

Families, individual characteristics and children's achievement: ethclass group differences

In the following analysis many of the different aspects of the study that have been discussed previously are brought together by adopting an interactionism model of children's achievements. As revealed in Chapter 1, the model being used takes the statistical form:

$$Z = aX + bY + cXY + dX^2 + eY^2 + \text{constant}$$

where Z, X and Y represent measures of academic performance, individual characteristics and family learning environments, respectively. Also, in Chapter 1, it was indicated that in formulating a general interactionism model, Thomas and Znaniecki (1958) proposed that in the field of social reality an effect, whether individual or social, always has a composite cause. Such a cause is considered to contain the subjective social-psychological elements of social reality (attitudes) and the objective social elements that impose themselves upon individuals and provoke their reactions (social values). It is suggested that there can be no change of social reality which is not the common effect of pre-existing social values and attitudes acting upon them, nor any change in individual consciousness which is not the common effect of pre-existing attitudes and social values acting upon them. That is, 'the cause of a value or an attitude is never an attitude or value alone, but always a combination of an attitude and a value' (Thomas, 1966: 277). The framework developed by Thomas and Znaniecki is adopted in the present section of the chapter to investigate relations between families, children's attitudes to school and academic achievement. Also, the theoretical perspective is loosened to include within the category of 'attitudes' a measure of children's intelligence. Thus, the following analysis is guided by the research questions, to what extent are measures of children's intelligence and school-related attitudes related to academic achievement scores at different levels of the learning environment of the family? As Thomas (1966: 274) warns

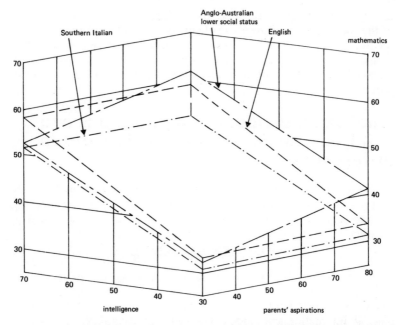

Figure 5.7 Fitted-mathematics scores in relation to parents' aspirations and intelligence

Even if we find that all the members of a social group react in the same way to a certain value, still we cannot assume that this value alone is the cause of this reaction, for the latter is also conditioned by the uniformity of attitudes prevailing in the group; and this uniformity cannot be taken as granted or omitted.

From all of the regression models that could have been used to examine the data of the study, the following representative frameworks are adopted to generate regression surfaces.
1. f(aspirations, intelligence) → mathematics
2. f(press for English, intelligence) → word knowledge
3. f(instrumental orientation scale, academic adjustment to school) → mathematics

f*(aspirations, intelligence)* → *mathematics*

The regression-fitted surfaces in Figure 5.7 show relations between intelligence test scores and mathematics performance at different levels of parents' aspirations. For the Anglo-Australian lower social-status children, intelligence and parents' aspirations both have significant linear associations with mathematics. At each level of intelligence, increases in the parents' aspiration scores from a low of thirty to a high of eighty, are associated with a regression-fitted mathematics increase of approximately ten points. Also, as the ability scores increase from standard values of thirty to seventy, the regression-fitted mathematics performance increases by approximately twenty points at each level of parents' aspirations. The surfaces for the English and Southern Italian children reflect the findings of many previous studies, suggesting that academic achievement is not related to the social environment of children with equal intellectual ability (also, see Chapter 3). For both the English and Southern Italian children, increases in intelligence scores from thirty to seventy are related to quite sizeable increments in mathematics achievement, at each aspiration level. Again, these regression surfaces show the great diversity of relations between the variables in the study, for children within different ethclasses.

f(press for English, intelligence) → word knowledge

The diversity of relationships between the variables is further emphasised by the shapes of the surfaces depicted in Figure 5.8, which show the regression-fitted associations between press for English and word knowledge at different levels of the Raven's test scores (also see Marjoribanks, 1979*d*). For the Anglo-Australian lower social-status children, the word knowledge scores have significant associations with both the intelligence and environment scores, while the plane for the Greek children reflects models in which academic achievement has linear relations to intelligence, at different environment levels, but where the criterion measures are not associated with the environment variables, at different levels of intelligence. The surface for Greek children may be a result of the very low mean press for English scores of Greek families and the truncated nature of the distribution of those scores, which may prevent the press values being 'active' in the regression models. For Southern Italian children the curvature of the surface reveals the complexity of relations that may exist between intelligence, family environment and academic performance. At each level of intelligence, increments in press for English scores are associated with quite sizeable increments in Southern Italian children's word knowledge performance until a ceiling of achievement appears to be approached. In Figure 5.8, the surfaces highlight the need to link investigations of children's academic achievement to the social circumstances of families and not only to family social-psychological

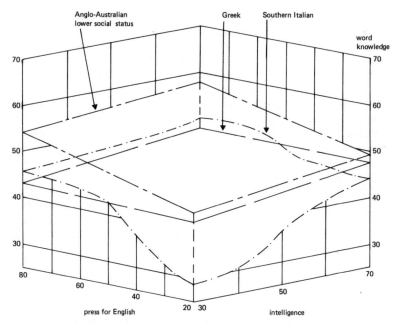

Figure 5.8 Fitted-word knowledge scores in relation to press for English and intelligence

variables. Also, the findings from Figures 5.7 and 5.8 support the assertion of Banks (1976: 69) that the controversies surrounding ethnic group differences in children's intellectual abilities are 'unlikely to be resolved until we have a much greater knowledge of the ways in which abilities develop in interaction with the environment.'

f *(instrumental orientation scale, academic adjustment to school) → mathematics*

In the final regression surface of the study, regression-fitted relations are presented between children's academic adjustment to school and mathematics performance at different levels of an instrumental orientation scale. The instrumental orientation scale consists of a combination of press for English and parents' achievement orientation scores. For Southern Italian children, in Figure 5.9, the environment and attitude scores both have significant linear associations with mathematics achievement, while for the Anglo-Australian lower

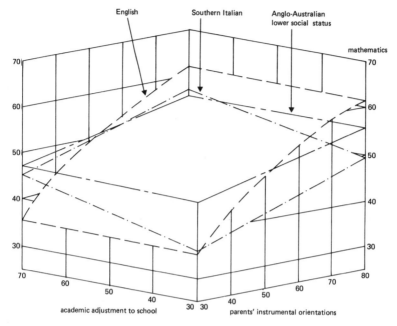

Figure 5.9 Fitted-mathematics scores in relation to instrumental orientations and academic adjustment to school

social-status and English children the attitude values are not related to mathematics performance, at different family environment levels. These latter findings provide only partial support for the conceptual framework suggesting that children's attitudes will be related to academic performance at different levels of family learning environments. It is possible that in the lower social-status Anglo families, a restricted variation in family environment scores may prevent the attitudes from being associated with achievement in a 'predictable' manner. For example, Thomas (1966: 20) proposes that the more uniform and steady the social influences are on an individual, the more difficult it is for the individual 'to find around him influences which would make him take a course different from other members of the group in acquiring a new attitude. Of course this means also a limitation of the variety of possible attitudes and values that can develop from a given starting-point.'

Typically, the findings from an analysis of the interactionism model show that the two measures of individual characteristics have differential relations to academic performance at different family environments, within the various ethclass groups. Again, the results indicate the need to adopt multiple measures of children's character- istics and environmental contexts if our understanding of children's development is to be enhanced (see Marjoribanks, 1978d).

The results that have been presented in this and in previous chapters indicate the complex nature of the correlates of children's school achievement, with the associations between measures of achievement, individual characteristics and families often being quite different between ethclasses. But it must be stressed again that the present analysis is restricted to an investigation of only one of the social contexts in which a child operates. Also, that social context has been assessed in relation to parents' interpretations. In the following chapter some policy implications of the research are examined, and while these implications concentrate on family contexts, the total conceptual thrust of the present analysis is in accord with the contention of Halsey (1975: 17) that

> The association of social class [and ethnicity] with educational achievement will not therefore be explained by a theory or elim- inated by a policy which falls short of including changes in public support for learning in the family neighbourhood, the training of teachers, the production of relevant curricula, the fostering of parental participation, the raising of standards of housing and employment prospects, and, above all, the allocation of educ- ational resources.

6

Family and School Interaction

One of the major recommendations of the 'Galbally' Report, commissioned by the Australian government to review post-arrival programmes and services for new Australian settlers, is to allocate additional funds for the teaching of English as a second language and for the development of multicultural educational programmes (Galbally Report, 1978). The recommendation is generated from statements indicating that, 'Because we recognise that migrants' knowledge of the English language is a critical factor in enabling successful settlement in Australia we give special attention to the teaching of English both to children and to adults' (1978: 7), and 'those who do not learn adequate English continue to be at a disadvantage and often suffer considerably in employment, through isolation from social contact and in many other ways' (1978: 5). After suggesting that action should be taken to construct new multicultural and English language programmes, the Report, however, observes that there is a 'dearth of information' available about what type of programmes should be established, which 'prevents us from specifying exactly where additional funds are needed and what activities already carried out in the school systems may be worthy of support' (1978: 40). Instead, broad educational goals such as the following are proposed

our schools and school systems should be encouraged to develop more rapidly various initiatives aimed at improving the understanding of the different histories, cultures, languages and attitudes of those who make up our society. This greater understanding can be achieved in a range of ways—for example through greater allocation of resources to the teaching of histories, cultures and languages (both English and other languages), through development of bilingual teaching, through better teacher education in these fields, both before and during teachers' active careers, through development of curriculums and essential materials and through greater involvement of parents and the community. (1978: 106.)

In an attempt to increase our understanding of the possible structure of school curriculum for children from non-Anglo eth-classes, the present chapter investigates parents' expectations of the types of programmes that might be established in 'multi-ethnic' schools. Also, policy implications of the research regarding parent-teacher interactions are considered.

Programmes in schools for non-Anglo children

In the family environment schedule (see Appendix A) questions were included to assess parents' opinions about the nature of school programmes that they considered should be offered to children from non-Anglo ethclasses. Responses to the questions are presented in the form of profiles of percentage scores. In the figures the three Anglo-group profiles are plotted adjacent to the parent scores for the three non-Anglo groups. Profiles, rather than Tables, have been chosen as the form of presentation, as it is considered they provide a clearer and more parsimonious description of the differences in responses within and between ethclasses. The first question that was asked related to general language teaching and was of the form:

When children, who are about 10 years old, arrive in Australia from non-English-speaking countries, into which of the following school situations do you think they should be placed?
A. In special schools set up to teach English to ethnic children.
B. The local school, but placed in special classes where the children spend most of their time learning English.
C. The local school and placed in ordinary classes, but with some special English teaching.
D. The local school and placed in ordinary classes with no special attention.
E. The local school but with the children taught mainly in their own language.

In Figure 6.1, the profiles show nearly identical patterns of parents' responses for the three Anglo ethclasses, while there is significant variation in parents' scores for the three non-Anglo ethclasses. Also, there are major differences between the profile shapes for Anglo and non-Anglo parents. Approximately 60 per cent of parents in the three Anglo groups, for example, suggest that the children should attend ordinary classes within local schools but also offered some special English teaching. The corresponding percentages for Greek, Southern

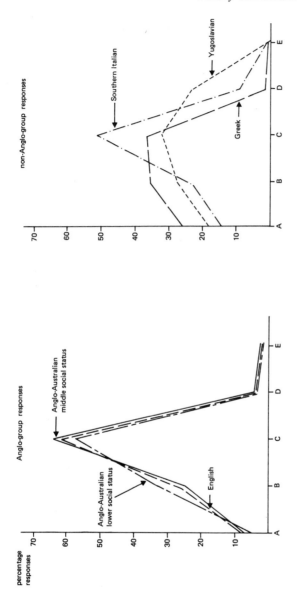

A : In special classes set up to teach English to ethnic children
B : The local school but placed in special classes where the children spend most of their time learning English
C : Local school and placed in ordinary classes but with some special English teaching
D : Local school and placed in ordinary classes with no special attention
E : Local school but with the children taught primarily in their own language

Figure 6.1 Profiles relating to general language-teaching situations

Italian, and Greek parents are 37, 52 and 32, respectively. If re-sponses to the alternatives A and B are added, then 61 per cent of Greek parents indicate that recently arrived non-Anglo 10-year-olds should be taught English primarily in special classes, either in special or local schools. For Southern Italian and Yugoslavian parents, however, only 38 and 45 per cent, respectively, support the possibility of such special treatment. In contrast, 23 per cent of Yugoslavian and 10 per cent of Southern Italian parents suggest that no special attention should be organised for the children, while only 2 per cent of Greek parents express such sentiments. In the Galbally Report (1978: 38) it is proposed that

> there is significant evidence to suggest that many migrant students do badly in reading and literacy tests and have difficulty with normal classroom lessons—attributable in most cases to difficulties in coping with the English language. The implications of difficulties with English remain with some students throughout their lives and limit their ability to participate in more advanced studies.

As a result, the Report (1978: 39) recommends that to increase the number of non-Anglo-group children receiving special English in-struction and in order to improve the quality of the instruction, extra funds should be used in a number of ways, including

(a) increasing the numbers of special teachers;
(b) improving the training of special teachers of English, and training classroom teachers in meeting the special needs of children of non-English speaking backgrounds;
(c) improving the production and distribution of teaching ma-terials, particularly to encourage further use of 'normal class' methods (as well as withdrawal into special classes) in meeting language needs.

By encouraging schools to use normal classrooms as the environ-ment for teaching English as a second language, complemented by the possible withdrawal of students into special English classrooms, the Report is in general sympathy with the opinions expressed in the present analysis by the Anglo, Southern Italian and Yugoslavian parents. There is less agreement, however, between the recommen-dation and the stated interests of Greek parents. Some of the group differences in language-teaching expectations are explored further in the following questions.

The second question in the schedule, relating to language teaching, was as follows:

When children start school at the age of 5 or 6 and they are from (non-English-speaking) ethnic families, in what language do you think the children should be taught?
A. Totally in their own language.
B. Mainly in their own language with some English.
C. About half English and half in the ethnic language.
D. Mainly English and some ethnic language.
E. All English.

The question was asked in two sections: first, for children who had just arrived in Australia, and second, in relation to children who had been in Australia for most of their lives. Parents' responses relating to recently arrived young children are shown in the profiles in Figure 6.2, while responses referring to children who have lived in Australia for most of their lives are presented in Figure 6.3. The profiles in Figure 6.2 reveal that more Anglo-group than non-Anglo-group parents are in favour of a curriculum for the 6-year-olds that is taught primarily in the language of the child. Approximately 12 per cent of parents from the two Anglo-Australian ethclasses and 21 per cent of English parents respond that the newly arrived 6-year-olds should be taught either 'totally in their own language' or 'mainly in their own language with some English'. In contrast, only about 5 per cent of parents from each of the non-Anglo groups support the two 'primarily ethnic language' alternatives. Over a quarter of the parents in each of the Anglo groups suggest that the children should be taught totally in English, while the corresponding percentages for Greek, Southern Italian and Yugoslavian families are 18, 22 and 59, respectively. Generally, the findings indicate again the variation, between and within ethclasses, in parents' educational attitudes and expectations. If a bilingual teaching context is defined as one attempting to give equal or nearly equal importance to two languages as the medium of instruction, then the percentage of Greek, Southern Italian and Yugoslavian parents supporting such an orientation are 33, 38 and 36, respectively. The corresponding percentage support for a bilingual programme from the Anglo parents is: Anglo-Australian middle social status, 36; Anglo-Australian lower social status, 32; and, English, 22 per cent. It probably needs to be reasserted that the findings of the analysis must be interpreted within the limitations associated with using a family environment interview schedule. Results from such schedules can provide only a partial understanding of social situations. Ethnographic analyses of families from different Australian ethclasses are required to embellish the conclusions of the present investigation.

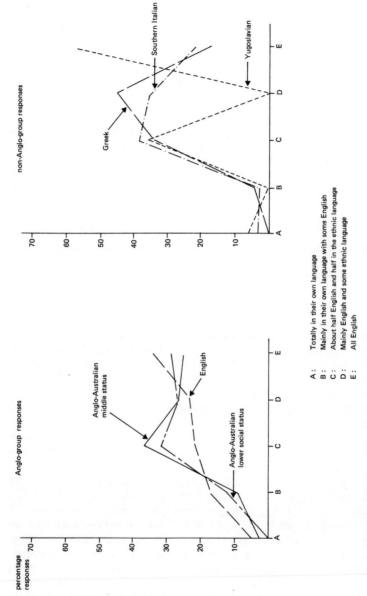

A : Totally in their own language
B : Mainly in their own language with some English
C : About half English and half in the ethnic language
D : Mainly English and some ethnic language
E : All English

Figure 6.2 Parents' language-teaching expectations: 6-year-old recently arrived non-Anglo children

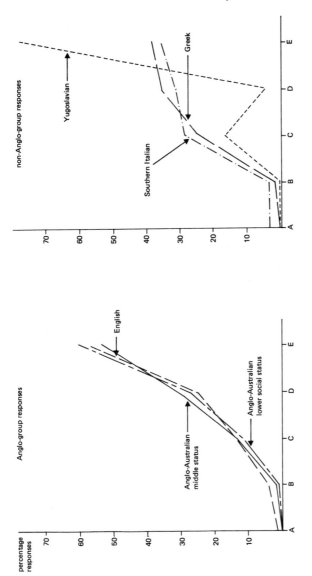

A : Totally in their own language
B : Mainly in their own language with some English
C : About half English and half in the ethnic language
D : Mainly English and some ethnic language
E : All English

Figure 6.3   Parents' language-teaching expectations: 6-year-old longer-term resident children

As indicated earlier, the question analysed in Figure 6.2 was repeated for 6-year-olds who had lived in Australia most of their lives. For both variations of the question, the same set of possible answers were supplied by the interviewer so that any changes in parents' responses could be observed. The comparative analysis of parents' replies were guided by the following two propositions:

(a) The longer non-Anglo-group children are resident in Australia, the more likely that Anglo-group parents will suggest curriculum alternatives for those children that are taught primarily or totally in English.

(b) The stronger the desires of non-Anglo-group parents to have their children learn the language of their ethnic group, the more likely that the parents will suggest curriculum alternatives for their children that are taught primarily or partly in the ethnic language.

Generally, the shapes of the profiles for the Anglo-group families in Figures 6.2 and 6.3 provide support for the first proposition. Quite clearly, the profiles representing Anglo-group parents' responses for 6-year-olds who have been in Australia for most of their lives are displaced well to the right, when compared to the profiles relating to recently arrived children. For example, in Anglo-Australian middle social status, Anglo-Australian lower social status and English families, the percentages of parents suggesting that the 6-year-olds should be taught either 'totally in English' or 'mainly English and some ethnic language' are 85 (52), 88 (56) and 83 (57), respectively, with the figures for recently arrived children in parentheses.

The second proposition suggests a positive relationship between parents' desires to have their children learn the language of the ethnic group and their expectations of having part of the school curriculum taught in their ethnic language. When non-Anglo-group parents were asked 'How important is it to you that the language of your ethnic group should be maintained within the family and that your child should speak it fluently?', 36, 50 and 14 per cent of Greek, Southern Italian and Yugoslavian parents, respectively, responded that it was 'extremely important', while the corresponding group percentages indicating that it was 'important' were 59, 42 and 37. Only for the Yugoslavians was there a large group of parents (41 per cent) who replied that it was 'not really important' or they 'don't care' (8 per cent). Also, when parents were asked 'how particular are you about the way your child speaks the ethnic language of the family?' the following percentages of parents indicated they were 'very strict' or 'quite particular': Greek, 72; Southern Italian, 75; and Yugoslavian,

50. Parents expressing that they were 'not too particular' or 'don't really care' were: Greek, 28; Southern Italian, 25; and Yugoslavian, 36 per cent. In relation to the second proposition, the strong desire by Greek and Southern Italian parents, in particular, to maintain their languages within families suggests that a significant proportion of parents from those two ethclasses will express a desire to have part of the teaching within schools to be conducted in their own languages. From Figures 6.2 and 6.3, the percentages of non-Anglo parents responding that the curriculum should be taught 'totally in the child's language', 'mainly in the child's language with some English' or 'half in English and half in the ethnic language' for 6-year-olds are: Greek, 27 (37); Southern Italian, 33 (43); and Yugoslavian, 18 (41), with the figures in parentheses relating to new immigrant children. That is, an educationally significant proportion of non-Anglo parents express support for a curriculum orientation in which English is not the dominant medium of instruction for children starting school. Compared to the other non-Anglo groups, Yugoslavian parents expressed a weaker desire to retain the 'ethnic' language in the family and they indicated stronger support for the teaching of their children in English. These initial analyses provide general support for the second proposition.

In a further and perhaps more stringent test of the two propositions the following question, which is similar in format to the previous one, was asked:

When children from (non-Anglo Australian) ethnic families have reached the age of about ten or eleven, in what language do you think they should be taught at school?

Again the question related to children who had just arrived in Australia, and for those who had been in Australia for most of their lives. The possible responses supplied by the interviewer were identical to those of the previous question for 6-year-olds.

The profiles in Figures 6.4 and 6.5 reveal that the percentages of Anglo-group parents suggesting that the 11-year-olds should be taught either 'totally in English' or 'mainly in English with some ethnic language' are: Anglo-Australian middle social status, 60 (55); Anglo-Australian lower status, 95 (57); and English, 99 (62), with the figures in parentheses for newly arrived immigrant children. Again, these data support the proposition that the longer ethclass group children are resident in Australia, the weaker will be the Anglo-group parents' support for bilingual education programmes. In particular, the proposition is supported strongly for the Anglo lower status parents. For example, 76 per cent of English parents and 73 per cent

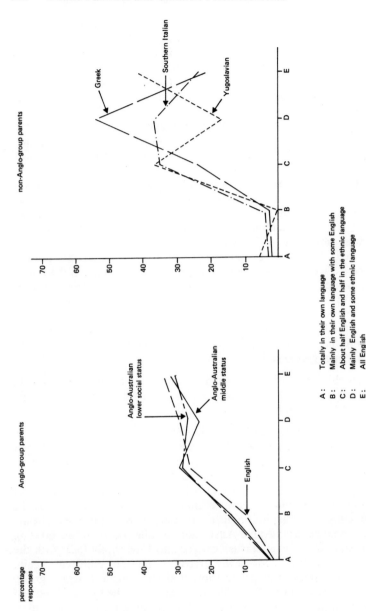

Figure 6.4 Parents' language-teaching expectations: 11-year-old recently arrived non-Anglo children

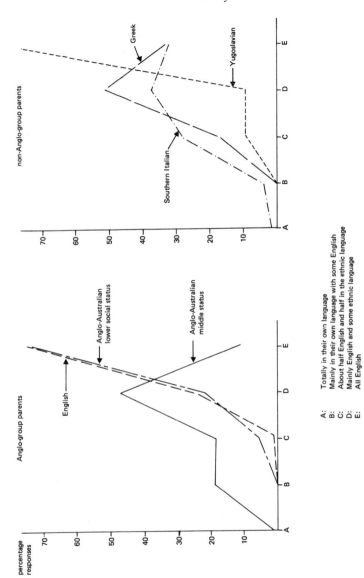

Figure 6.5 Parents' language teaching expectations: 11-year-old longer term resident children

of Anglo-Australian lower social-status parents suggest that the curriculum for the 11-year-olds who have lived in Australia for most of their lives should be taught totally in English, while only 12 per cent of the Anglo middle social-status parents agree with such an alternative. It should be noted that generally, the lower social-status Anglo-Australian and English children in the sample attended 'multi-ethnic' schools, while the middle social-status children attended schools with very few non-Anglo-group children. Therefore, the middle social-status parents are expressing sentiments about schools to which they do not send their children and as a result their responses must be interpreted within the limitations of that social situation.

When the profiles in Figures 6.3 and 6.5 are compared, for Anglo-group parents, they provide partial support for the first proposition. The profiles reveal that the proportion of lower social-status parents responding in favour of a greater component of English teaching in the curriculum, for children who have resided in Australia for most of their lives, is greater for 11-year-olds than for 6-year-olds. Middle social-status parents' responses reflect an opposite trend.

The previous analysis of the second proposition indicates that it may be restated to suggest that, compared to Yugoslavian families, Southern Italian and Greek parents will express stronger support for 'bilingual' programmes for 11-year-old children. In Figures 6.4 and 6.5, the percentages of non-Anglo parents suggesting that the teaching of 11-year-olds should be conducted either 'totally in the child's language', 'mainly in the child's language', or 'half in English and half in the ethnic language' are: Greek, 17 (26); Southern Italian, 32 (40); and Yugoslavian, 9 (41), with the figures in parentheses for new immigrant children. Again these figures show that for Southern Italians, in particular, a significant proportion of parents support a 'bilingual' school programme. The weaker Greek support for such a curriculum may reflect the alternative programmes that the Greek community organised for children in the present sample. Most of the Greek children attended Greek language and Greek culture courses as out-of-school activities. Thus while Greek parents generally stress strong desires to maintain Greek within the family, most of the parents may judge that the extra-school programmes satisfy their expectations for the teaching of Greek language.

Typically, the parents in the study from the lower social-status Anglo families and the Yugoslavian group provide only moderate support for 'bilingual' education programmes for non-Anglo children approaching the end of elementary school, especially if the children have lived in Australia for most of their lives. Although a majority of middle social-status Southern Italian and Greek parents do not indicate support for a bilingual programme, there is nonetheless a significant number of parents from these groups who do support such an orientation to the curriculum. Also, the findings reveal that acceptance of such programmes increases for younger children and also for children if they are recent arrivals. Such conclusions have a number of important policy implications. First, if schools consider that a 'bilingual' or 'primarily ethnic-language' programme is educationally desirable for children from non-Anglo families, then teachers need to convince many non-Anglo, as well as Anglo, parents of the advantages of such a curriculum. Second, because of the diversity of parents' responses, within and between ethclasses, schools might be established that offer a curriculum in varying proportions of ethnic languages and English. Elementary schools, for example, might offer: (a) an ethnic language programme in which the medium of instruction is, say, 80 per cent in an ethnic language with the remainder in English, (b) a bilingual programme giving equal status to English and an ethnic language in classroom teaching, (c) a predominantly English orientation where, perhaps, 80 per cent of instruction is provided in English and 20 per cent in an ethnic language, and (d) a programme in which all the instruction is offered in English. Parents could then be given the choice of that school, or that programme within a school, which approximated their educational expectations. In such a proposal it is important to stress that Anglo-group parents should be offered the possibility of enrolling their children in programmes where English is not the only, or even major, medium of instruction. Later in the chapter an experiment is discussed in which English-speaking parents organised a predominantly French language curriculum for their children.

If a policy of establishing alternative-language learning environments was adopted it would not, of course, be feasible to offer programmes in all the languages represented in Australian elementary schools. Unfortunately, economic restrictions would allow only those languages of the most numerical ethclasses and the international languages to be provided. Organisationally, the alternative language orientations could be located either in the same school or within a consortium of neighbouring schools, with teachers being attached to the consortium rather than to individual institutions. The adoption of an educational policy that recognises the cultural and linguistic pluralism of children may be one of the most significant factors in creating an harmonious multicultural Australian society. As the Bullock Report (1975: 294) suggests, schools should recognise that the bilingualism of immigrant children is of great importance to the children and their families, and also to society as a whole ... Certainly the school should adopt a positive attitude to its pupils' bilingualism and wherever possible should help maintain and deepen their knowledge of their mother-tongues. The school that really welcomes its immigrant parents must also be prepared to welcome their languages ... In any event, bilingual pupils should be encouraged to maintain their mother-tongue throughout their schooling.

Questions that have been examined so far in this chapter relate directly to language teaching in schools. The final question for parents was related to the general content of curriculum and asked:

If a school has a large number of children from non-English-speaking countries, how much time in grades four and five should be devoted to teaching about the history, geography, culture, languages, ... of those countries?

A. All subjects should be related to 'ethnic-countries' with little or no attention to Australia.

B. Mainly related to 'ethnic-countries' with a reasonable amount of Australian history, geography, ...

C. About half related to 'ethnic-countries' and half to Australia.

D. Mainly devoted to Australia with some time devoted to 'ethnic-countries'.

E. All the time should be devoted to the study of Australia or other English-speaking countries.

The profiles in Figure 6.6 show some similarities in responses between Anglo and non-Anglo-group parents. Approximately 65 per cent of the Anglo parents, for example, favour alternatives D or E, while 50-55 per cent of non-Anglo-group parents express similar sentiments. Both profiles show that a significant proportion of parents support the alternative that half the general curriculum should relate to 'ethnic-countries' and half to Australia. As in the analysis of the previous questions in this chapter, the responses depicted in Figure 6.6 show the great variation, within ethclasses, of parents' expectations about certain aspects of their children's schooling.

From the investigations of the questions that have been presented, it is obvious that educators must not assume that parents from the same, or different, ethclass will have similar educational concerns. Only after consultation with parents can there be a movement towards achieving programmes that reflect the 'right' mix of teachers' educational knowledge and parents' expectations. If such pro-grammes are to be achieved, then classroom teachers must be given

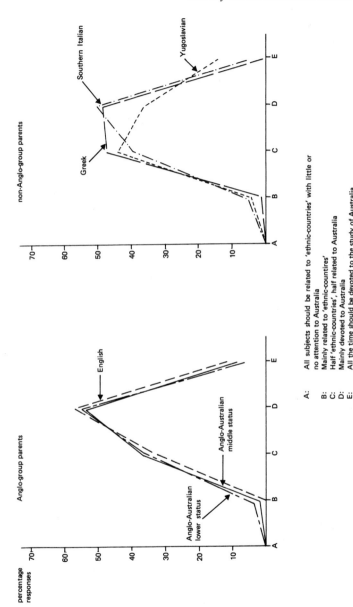

A: All subjects should be related to 'ethnic-countries' with little or
     no attention to Australia
B: Mainly related to 'ethnic-countires'
C: Half 'ethnic-countries', half related to Australia
D: Mainly devoted to Australia
E: All the time should be devoted to the study of Australia

Figure 6.6   Profiles of parents' general curriculum expectations

the opportunity of always being familiar with the latest significant academic and pedagogic developments in curriculum and they must always be sensitive to, and understanding of, parents' opinions. For example, when teachers choose conceptual frameworks on which to construct language programmes for non-Anglo children, it is important that they differentiate between frameworks that support the design of bilingual programmes from those that generate bidialectical curriculum. In an examination of non-standard Negro English (NNE) and standard English (SE), for example, Labov (1968: 345) proposes that the

> Problems of teaching English to speakers of Italian are of a different order from those of teaching the rules of SE and NNE speakers. The Italian speakers have no fixed rules of English structure, but the NNE students have already internalized a set of English rules from earliest childhood.

It may not be completely accurate to suggest that non-Anglo children who settled in Australia at an early age, who live in non-English-speaking families but who are taught in English-speaking classrooms, do not develop their own form of an English dialect. But the general caveat being offered is that when teachers construct learning experiences for non-Anglo and Anglo-group children, they need to be aware of the appropriate conceptual frameworks. The delicacy required in establishing relations between teachers and parents is expressed in the Bullock Report (1975: 59), when it is suggested that

> They [the parents] do not recognise their own potential in furthering his educational development, and not uncommonly they are apprehensive that any attempt to teach him or introduce him to books will conflict with the school's methods and thus confuse him. Moreover, there may be the natural suspicion on the part of the mother that a home visitor is bringing with her a critical attitude to the child's upbringing or the conditions of the home ... All this makes it an exercise requiring great tact and particular qualities on the part of the visitor ... The visitor will have to be tolerant and understanding, imposing no judgment and hinting no censure.

In the following section of the chapter a number of programmes that have been successful in establishing parent-school relationships are examined.

Parent-school interaction

The analyses of the present study indicate once again the important relationships that exist between family learning environments and children's academic performance. But the research also emphasises the differential nature of those relations within and between eth-classes. As indicated in the previous section of the chapter, if teachers are to organise meaningful learning environments for children, then they need to develop a curriculum that reflects the varying expectations and circumstances of parents and also their own educational knowledge. Therefore, the creation of positive parent-teacher relationships should be a goal of all schools that are attempting to construct stimulating classroom learning situations. As Midwinter (1977: 22) suggests

> Whatever else home-school relations have achieved during the last decade, one absolute truth has been revealed. Most (not all, but most) parents are vitally concerned about their children's education, and *provided the school and the teachers are prepared to adapt the character of their home-school links to the character of the parents' subculture*, they will respond diligently.

In the present section of the chapter, research related to parent-teacher interaction is examined. An analysis of the many programmes that have been attempted is not provided, as reviews of the research exist already (e.g. Little and Smith, 1972; Bronfenbrenner, 1974; Pilling and Kellmer Pringle, 1978). Instead, two programmes are selected for discussion: first, the Educational Priority Area projects of England and Scotland, in which schools were the main initiators of parent-teacher links; and second, the St Lambert experiment of bilingual education in Canada, where parents were responsible for organising a new curriculum for their children.

Educational priority area projects: parents and schools

In the publication of the Plowden Report (1967) entitled, *Children and their Primary Schools*, it was suggested that a programme of positive discrimination should be adopted to make schools in the most socially deprived areas of England as good as the best in the country. As a result of the recommendations of the Report, an action-research framework was adopted to guide the development and evaluation of educational programmes in designated 'educational priority areas' in parts of London, Birmingham, Liverpool and the West Riding. A parallel Scottish project was undertaken in Dundee. The general objectives of the action programme were

(a) to raise the educational performance of the children;
(b) to improve the morale of teachers;
(c) to increase the involvement of parents in their children's education; and
(d) to increase the 'sense of responsibility' for their communities of the people living in them.

(Halsey, 1972: 57.)

That is, a major concern of the programmes was 'to encourage parents to recognise their own role in the educational process and so to develop understanding, skill and enthusiasm in the children's homes which would help them to get the maximum benefit from their schools' (Halsey, 1972: 117). But Halsey also suggests that, 'not only must parents understand schools, schools must also understand the families and environments in which the children live' (1972: 117). In the implementation of the programmes it was hoped that schools would adopt complementary rather than compensatory stances to families, so that rather than implicitly opposing the values of the community, schools could attempt to understand and come to terms with them. An implication of the orientation adopted by the priority programmes, for the present study, is that if Australian schools are to create complementary school environments that are in harmony with the home, then they must understand the differential family environments that are created by parents within and between ethclasses. If harmonious complementary relationships are not developed, then schools may increasingly become divisive forces separating children from their families. It is important to stress that constructing parent-teacher links should not be restricted to lower social-status parents. As Midwinter (1977: 52) observes

The object of these exercises, [is], to give the parents the fairest balance of self assurance and educational information for them to support their children's efforts in school. And that might mean persuading the university-educated professional man of the benefits of learning through play, as well as explaining to the harassed working mother the benefits for her son [or daughter] if he [she] were to stay on at school.

Generally, the aim of the parent-school programmes in the priority projects was to bring parents into the school and to take education to the home. The methods adopted in the different action-research approaches are described in detail in Halsey (1972), Morrison (1974), Barnes (1975), and Smith (1975).

After his experiences with the Liverpool project, Midwinter (1975: 62) suggests that parent-teacher relationships may develop through two separate phases. During the initial phase it is proposed that teachers and parents build up a working social relationship. Such relationships are generated as the result of parents being invited to the schools or teachers visiting homes, after which teachers and parents become aware of each others concern for particular children's education. The different priority projects used a combination of means to develop such social relationships, including: the use of publications directed at parents, organising children's exhibitions and live demonstrations within community settings as well at school, the involvement of parents with their children in classroom learning activities, undertaking school-community environmental improvement schemes, and the use of a home-liason teacher who, 'is concerned partly with explaining the aims and methods of the schools so that parents can better understand the nature of the experience their children receive within them, and partly with encouraging parents to have confidence in their own capacity to teach' (Halsey, 1972: 191). It is claimed by Halsey that 'it is of the first importance that this kind of home-school work should be the responsibility of qualified teachers who have a thorough understanding of pedagogical methods and of the special challenge presented by the educational priority areas' (1972: 191).

While many of the priority schools recorded successes in fostering positive parent-teacher social relationships, there were also disappointing experiences. In a school in the Dundee programme, for example, Watt (1974: 7) indicates that

> the most frustrating example was in the efforts of a group of young mothers who had been associated with E.P.A. playgroups and, finding great satisfaction in their association with the mothers' club there, wished to extend this relationship to the primary schools and initiate an informal club there when their children were at statutory school age. Despite these mothers showing such an active interest in their children's education and despite their willingness to be actively involved in the school, the scheme came to nothing largely because the schools were unwilling to accept that parents should play what to them was an unconventional role. In all schools there were those who, while accepting that parents had a broad role within the system, saw that role as essentially 'submissive',...

Failures such as that in the Dundee situation, and in others where teachers have suggested that parents show a lack of interest in their child's schooling, have prompted Midwinter (1977: 21–22) to claim that for the development of 'phase one' parent-teacher social relationships, 'If the host community is to have free and fluid communion with the school, then the media for that communion must fall naturally and spontaneously and comfortably within the social and cultural purview of the parents.' He then suggests, 'What has been too easily labelled "apathy" in the past has often been no more than the wrong brand of invitation failing. Teachers have blamed parents for being lethargic rather than themselves for being insensitive and insufficiently gifted in public relations.'

In the 'second phase' of parent-teacher interaction, Midwinter (1975) proposes that teachers need to adopt the role of 'educational visitor' where they take the 'classroom to the doorstep'. He suggests that the teacher must bring the parent into a dialogue, 'not so much as a teaching aide, rather as a partner, even a learner, in the process ... We must move beyond the cosy practices of home-school relations and, in a phrase, get down to a hard, solid campaign of parental education, that our children may be better educated' (1975: 62). A 'Home Visiting Project' was included as part of the West Riding priority scheme, in which educational visitors created a home learning programme related to pre-school children. The aims of the scheme were to

> (1) study the educational environment of young children, particularly the mother-child relationship; (2) examine the stages of development in children's play and learning in the home; (3) try to discover in co-operation with the mother any problems or difficulties in the child's progress; (4) work out a programme acceptable to individuals and families in the community whereby these problems could be overcome. (Smith, 1975: 138.)

The description of the study indicates that, initially, not all mothers were enthusiastic about the programme, with many being suspicious that it might be critical of their child-rearing methods. Mothers had to be convinced that the purpose of the visiting was to form a teaching partnership between the visitor and the mother, for the child. But as well as adopting a teaching role, the visitors state that it is 'necessary to be aware of the family's wider circumstances ... it is such economic and social factors which influence the relationships within the home .... A programme which ignores these problems, and concentrates on strictly educational activities, will have little long term effect' (Smith, 1975: 156–57).

Thus in 'phase one' of school-home interactions, attempts are made to establish positive social relationships reflecting mutual respect by teachers and parents. In 'phase two' the task of educational visitors is to encourage and reinforce parents in their educative role. The transition between the adoption of the two phases involves major educational decisions for schools. In the present study, the findings imply that if ethclass group differences in children's mean academic achievement are to be reduced, then policies implementing school-home teaching partnerships might be required. It was stated in Chapter 1 that 'because of the realities of the distribution of power in society, certain ethclasses are disadvantaged in relation to the creation of learning environments associated with those achievements rewarded in society' (p. 20). Although the mean parents' aspiration scores for non-Anglo ethclass families are high, the study shows that many of the families do not provide a supportive academically oriented or 'committed' learning environment. While reduction in ethclass group differences in children's achievements may be achieved by schools creating varying forms of 'bilingual' education programmes, or adopting other curriculum alternatives, it is probable that such strategies will need to be augmented by the development of parent-teacher partnerships in which teachers assist, in particular, non-Anglo parents with their English learning and help all parents create more academically oriented learning environments. That is, attempts should be made to weaken the association between family social circumstances and the cultural capital that can be transmitted to children by families. The present research agrees with the Galbally Report (1978: 4) that, in Australia, 'every person should be able to maintain his or her culture without prejudice or disadvantage and should be encouraged to understand and embrace other cultures'. If non-Anglo and lower social-status Anglo-Australian parents are to become more effective in providing a 'committed' learning environment, as defined in this study, then educational visitors may provide the means by which parents increase their own 'teaching' skills and also learn about the educative processes of school systems.

The Educational Priority Area programme provides a documented example of the difficulties and rewards associated with establishing parent-teacher interactions. In the projects the initiatives for developing relationships were taken generally by teachers. The second example of parent-school relations is chosen because it involved parents approaching a school system to organise a new curriculum. Also, the study is relevant to the present research as it concerns bilingual education.

The St Lambert experiment

The St Lambert experiment was developed in response to a group of English-speaking middle social-status parents in Quebec who wanted to know what would happen to children if they attended elementary schools where French rather than English was the major medium of instruction. In the report of the research, Lambert and Tucker (1972: 221) indicate that the parents wanted to give their children 'early training in the second language before stereotypes and prejudices had a chance to form, and to take advantage of the young child's apparent ease in language learning'. To achieve their goals parents wanted a French language programme developed in kindergarten and for the first three years of elementary school, within the English-speaking Protestant school system. After a series of rejections from school authorities, the parents organised a French programme for their children 'with the parents carrying the full load, both financially and pedagogically'. The parents then achieved political representation on the local school Board and organised meetings to discuss their proposals with other parents. After a press campaign and persistent representations to educational authorities, the group was eventually granted permission for a programme. The experiences of the St Lambert families indicate the need for parents to be familiar with the language and institutional processes of the mainstream social group if authority relationships are to be successfully challenged. That is why in the present study it has been suggested, on a number of occasions, that parents and children from minority power social groups should be aided in acquiring those aspects of family cultural capital that are associated with children's achievement. Unless parents and children attain the skills rewarded by society they are likely to remain 'disadvantaged'. Lambert and Tucker (1972: 226) claim, for example, that the parents perceived that the educational authorities accepted their proposals, 'not through any conviction of their own, but because the pressures on them were more than they could resist'.

Throughout the experiment the progress of children was monitored by researchers from the University of McGill. The close liason between the university and parents suggests a possible model for research within the Australian context. That is, universities and other tertiary institutions might increasingly form a link between parents, schools, educational authorities and the community in helping them to formulate new educational structures. The organisational success of the group in St Lambert is reflected in the comment by Lambert and Tucker (1972: 236) that it may be said with certainty that a small group of parents, by virtue of developing certain persuasive and intellectual skills, as well as by expending considerable energy, was able to effectuate a radical change in the curriculum of a conservative public school system.

In the evaluation of the research, the children's performance in the experimental group was compared with that of children from an English-only control group and a French-only control group. Children's achievements were adjusted statistically to take into account differences in performances on the Raven's Progressive Matrices and differences on a family environment schedule constructed from the frameworks suggested by Bloom (1964), Dave (1963), and Wolf (1964). At the end of first grade, the 'experimental' children who had been taught entirely in French were not retarded in their English development and their linguistic development in French progressed remarkably well. By the end of second grade, the third year of the scheme, the researchers claimed there were 'certain indicators of a beneficial enrichment of native-language development flowing from the bilingual experience' (Lambert and Tucker, 1972: 103), and that 'their abilities in spoken French are in many respects remarkable, although it is clear that at this stage they are not native-like in their command of oral French' (1972: 100). During the fourth year of the programme approximately 60 per cent of the teaching was in French with the remainder in English. By the end of that year the children showed 'no symptoms of retardation or negative transfer, and perform as well as the Controls on standard tests of English language competence,' (1972: 138) and achieve 'extremely well' (1972: 140) when compared to the French control group. The evaluators were able to claim that

> After five years, we are satisfied that the Experimental program has resulted in no native language or subject matter (i.e., arithmetic) deficit or retardation of any sort, nor is there any cognitive retardation attributable to participation in the program. In fact, the Experimental pupils appear to be able to read, write, speak, understand, and use English as competently as youngsters instructed in the conventional manner via English. During the same period of time and with no apparent personal or academic costs, the children have developed a competence in reading, writing, speaking, and understanding French that English pupils following a traditional French-as-a-Second-Language program for the same number of years could never match. (1972: 152.)

Although there are statistical limitations of the St Lambert experiment, such as small sample sizes, the programme has been discussed in detail, as it presents a possible schema for parents to adapt to the Australian context. It provides, for example, a case study for Anglo parents who may wish to have their children educated in a 'bilingual' curriculum and also a guide for non-Anglo families who would like their own ethnic language to form a significant part of a school's medium of instruction.

In the Educational Priority Projects and the St Lambert Experiment, the establishment of parent-school relations formed a major element in the structuring of the programmes. As schools become more aware of the educational impact of the different cultural capital available to children from different ethclasses, then the development of parent-teacher interactions that involve a teaching partnership, rather than reflecting primarily social relationships, are likely to be increasingly important in attempts to reduce educational inequalities. It is suggested by Midwinter (1977: 90), for example, that eventually

teachers will possibly all become adult educationists as well as child educationists, and that the borders of their work-pattern will be dictated rather more by the factors determining the children's education. The school will remain perhaps the focus or the headquarters or the hub of the enterprise, but it will cease to be regarded exclusively as the only agency where education can be sought or preferred.

Conclusion

In Weber's sociological analysis of social structures it is suggested that the ideal of the cultivated man adopted by a society is an outcome of the power of the dominant social group to universalise its particular cultural ideal. Generally, the present study provides support for two related general propositions derived from Weber's framework, *viz.*, (a) if dominant social groups have the power to determine what is valued in the educational system, then subordinate social groups will be 'disadvantaged' in relation to the criteria set by the more powerful groups and, more specifically, (b) families from certain ethclasses have the power to decide what is 'valued' in educational systems and these favoured groups have greater means of passing onto their children cultural capital related to the achievement of the valued goals of schooling.

Although ethclass group membership was associated with a moderate percentage of the variance in word knowledge and word comprehension scores, the ethclass group differences in intelligence were quite small. Intelligence was assessed using the Raven's Progressive Matrices and Jensen (1973*a*: 286) indicates that

> this non-verbal reasoning test . . . , is intended to be a pure measure of *g*, the general factor common to all intelligence tests. It is a highly reliable measure of reasoning ability, quite free of the influence of special abilities, such as verbal or numerical facility. It is probably the most culture-free test of general intelligence yet devised by psychologists.

The lack of overall group differences in the intelligence test scores should provide educators with confidence in the proposition that group differences in children's academic achievement can be reduced by restructuring learning environments. But the analysis of the regression surfaces throughout the research indicates that modest changes in family learning environments generally are associated with small increments in academic performance at different levels of children's individual characteristics. That is, a significant reduction in ethclass group differences in children's performances is likely to be related only to major changes in children's family, neighbourhood and school learning environments. For non-Anglo-Australian parents one of the most urgent requirements is the establishment of further programmes for the teaching of English. Press for English scores of Greek and Southern Italian parents, in particular, were quite low, with many of the parents indicating they were unable to assist their child with English.

Adult programmes in English that are developed should be taught in the context of social purpose, with the content and materials of the curriculum being related to that purpose. The social purpose for non-Anglo and lower social-status Anglo parents might be defined generally as the circumstances related to the education of children, so that programmes acquaint parents with the associations between social structure, the transmission of cultural capital through family and classroom learning environments, and children's potential educational attainments. Support for such a curriculum could be provided by governments, trade unions and employers. It is, for example, an unfortunate situation that so many employees in the lower social-status occupations in Australian universities, other tertiary institutions and schools are from non-Anglo ethclasses and unable to speak relatively fluently in the language of those institutions. Perhaps such educational organisations should arrange, within ordinary working hours, classes for adults who are not fluent in English. If such programmes were offered and were effective, then other organisations and industries might be encouraged to adopt the procedure. As well as attempting to assist parents, the findings suggest that schools might reorganise curriculum and allow more experimentation with the teaching of programmes in ethnic languages. It is realised, of course, that there are Australian schools and institutions already adopting innovatory language programmes for children and adults. What is being suggested now is that the findings of many of these programmes should be evaluated and that larger scale and more ambitious projects be undertaken.

If ethclass group differences in children's achievements are to be reduced, then the findings of the present analysis suggest that programmes need to be devised that incorporate action related to the family types that were developed in the typologies. The study has been purposely statistical as it was considered that such an orientation, using a relatively large number of families, would permit general propositions to be generated that could be tested by other investigators. If our knowledge of the inequalities in children's achievements is to be enhanced, then investigations are required that examine all the elements of the full conceptual model presented in Chapter 1. Only when we begin to compare the findings from studies using alternative theoretical and methodological approaches will our understandings of the structure of ethclass group differences in Australian children's achievements become increasingly revealed. At the moment our knowledge of the differences is very much like the understanding of the 'reader' in Guerard's analysis of the structure of impressionist novels, where he suggests

> One of the great beauties of impressionist structure lies in controlled movement, both musical and cinematic, toward revelation: the rhythms of changing, presently diminishing distance; of approach and withdrawal and reapproach; of shifts in lighting, with the verbal screens suddenly less opaque; of oblique and incremental allusion — the allusions understood by the novel's listener/thinker ... but not at first by the reader. (1976: 328.)

It is hoped that the present study has reduced the distance in our understanding of inequalities in Australian children's academic achievement.

Appendix A

Family Environment Schedule

The following interview schedule was used in the present research. It is presented for researchers who may wish to adapt it in studies assessing aspects of the social-psychological environments of families. The schedule and variations of it have been used in analyses of the environmental correlates of the cognitive and affective characteristics of Australian children (see Marjoribanks, 1979a). Therefore the wording needs to be adjusted for use within other national settings.

Part A provides general information about the family and an indication of how satisfied parents are with their child's schooling. In Part B, a number of social-psychological family environment variables are assessed.

Family Environment Interview Schedule

To the parents: The present set of questions are part of a study examining relationships that exist between families and the schools to which families send their children.

We would like to obtain some information from you regarding your feelings about the school your child (name the child) attends and to find out some of your thoughts about education in general. It is hoped that the kind of information that is collected in the study will be used by schools when they are planning their programmes.

The research guarantees anonymity of the family.

Request: It is essential to have a very accurate response to each question. However, if you feel that a question is an invasion of your privacy, feel free not to answer it. We would rather have no response to some questions than inaccurate responses. Your answers to the questions should be related to (name the child).

Thank you very much for your participation in the study.

The first set of questions deal with certain aspects of the family, in order to provide some general information for the study. Then the following questions are about your child (name the child) and the school she/he attends.

For the interviewer:
1. Each question should be asked of *all* parents, including Anglo-Australian parents, except where it is obvious from a previous answer that a question doesn't apply.

2. The questions are associated with numbers. Place a *circle* (not a tick) around the number which is closest to the answer supplied.
3. In the questionnaire, whenever X appears would you substitute the child's name.
4. An 'other answer' space is provided for most questions. If the responses that are given do not fit easily with the categories that are supplied, then write in the response. Also please supply any comments you feel might be useful when the schedule is being scored.
5. If after asking a question the parents have difficulty in providing an answer, then the interviewer should read out the possible alternatives that are provided.

Part A

1. Date of interview　_____
2. Surname of family　_____
3. First name of child　_____
4. Sex of child　　　M　　F　_____

5. Date of birth of child　_____
6. Home address　　_____
　　　　　　　　　_____
　　　　　　　　　_____
7. School attended by child　_____
8. Length of interview　_____
9. Who was interviewed
   (circle appropriate number)
   mother　　　　_____　1
   father　　　　_____　2
   both parents　　_____　3
   other (specify):　_____
10. In what country was the mother, father and X born?

	father	mother	child
Australia	1	2	3
Italy	1	2	3
Greece	1	2	3
Yugoslavia	1	2	3
Netherlands	1	2	3
Poland	1	2	3
England	1	2	3
Scotland	1	2	3
Northern Ireland	1	2	3
Wales	1	2	3
Eire	1	2	3
Germany	1	2	3

other country: name the country for:

father _____
mother _____
child _____

11. If the parents or child were not born in Australia, in what year did they arrive?
father _____
mother _____
child _____

12. What language is generally spoken in the home?
English 1
Italian 2
Greek 3
Dutch 4
German 5
Polish 6
other language (specify): _____

13. When you are speaking with X, what language would you use most of the time?

	father	mother
English	1	1
Italian	2	2
Greek	3	3
Dutch	4	4
German	5	5
Polish	6	6

other language (specify): _____

14. When X is talking with brothers or sisters or with other children in the home, what language does X generally use?
English 1
Italian 2
Greek 3
Dutch 4
German 5
Polish 6
other language (specify): _____

15. How satisfied would you say you are with the school that X attends?
very satisfied 1
reasonably satisfied 2
not really satisfied 3
very dissatisfied 4
don't know or don't care 5
other answer (specify): _____

16. How do you react to the following statements about X's school: would you agree strongly (1), agree (2), don't know (3), disagree (4), disagree strongly (5)?
In the school X attends:

		agree strongly	agree	don't know	disagree	disagree strongly
(a)	There is not enough homework	1	2	3	4	5
(b)	There is not enough discipline	1	2	3	4	5
(c)	Children are very friendly	1	2	3	4	5
(d)	Too much time is spent on subjects such as art, music, drama	1	2	3	4	5
(e)	Not enough time is spent on reading and mathematics	1	2	3	4	5
(f)	Teachers are very friendly	1	2	3	4	5
(g)	Teachers seem to treat all children very fairly	1	2	3	4	5
(h)	Teachers seem to be very interested in X's education	1	2	3	4	5
(i)	The methods of teaching seem to be too progressive, too modern	1	2	3	4	5
(j)	Too much time is spent on special courses for migrant children	1	2	3	4	5
(k)	Teachers give impression that they want to keep parents out of the school	1	2	3	4	5
(l)	Children from different ethnic groups mix very well	1	2	3	4	5
(m)	We don't receive enough information about how X is performing at her/his schoolwork	1	2	3	4	5

17. When children, who are about 10 years old, arrive in Australia from non-English-speaking countries, into which of the following school situations do you think they should be placed? (Ask all questions of Anglo-Australian parents as well.)

Read the following alternatives:

(a) In special schools set up to teach English to ethnic children   1
(b) The local school, but placed in special classes where the children spend most of their time learning English   2
(c) The local school and placed in ordinary classes, but with some special English teaching   3
(d) The local school and placed in ordinary classes with no special attention   4
(e) The local school, but with the children taught mainly in their own language   5

other answer (specify): ─────────────────────────

18. When children start school at the age of 5 or 6 and they are from (non-Anglo-Australian) ethnic families, in what language do you think the children should be taught? (Ask the question in two sections: first in relation to children who have just arrived in Australia, and second for children who have been in Australia for most of their lives.)
Read the alternatives:

	For children just arrived	For children resident in Australia for some time
(a) Totally in their own language	1	1
(b) Mainly in their own language with some English	2	2
(c) About half English and half in the ethnic language	3	3
(d) Mainly English and some ethnic language	4	4
(e) All English	5	5

other answer (specify): ——————————————————————

19. When children from (non-Anglo-Australian) ethnic families have reached the age of about 10 or 11, in what language do you think they should be taught in at school? (Ask the question in two sections: first in relation to children who have just arrived in Australia, and second for children who have been in Australia for most of their lives.)
Read the alternatives:

	For children just arrived	For children resident in Australia for some time
(a) Totally in their own language	1	1
(b) Mainly in their own language with some English	2	2
(c) About half English and half in the ethnic language	3	3
(d) Mainly English and some ethnic language	4	4
(e) All English	5	5

other answer (specify): ——————————————————————

20. If a school has a large number of children from non-English-speaking countries, how much time in grades 4 and 5 should be devoted to teaching about the history, geography, culture, languages, ... of those countries?
Read the alternatives:
(a) All such subjects should be related to ethnic countries, with little or no attention to Australia   1
(b) Mainly related to ethnic countries, with a reasonable amount of Australian history, geography   2

(c) About half related to ethnic countries and half to Australia　　3
(d) Mainly related to Australia, with some time devoted to ethnic
　　countries　　4
(e) All the time should be devoted to the study of Australia or
　　other English-speaking cultures　　5
other answer (specify): ————————————————————

21. At X's school, from what you know, how would you rate the teaching of the following subjects (either, very good (1), good (2), don't know (3), poor (4), very poor (5))?

	very good	good	don't know	poor	very poor
(a) Mathematics	1	2	3	4	5
(b) Reading	1	2	3	4	5
(c) English	1	2	3	4	5
(d) Sports	1	2	3	4	5
(e) Social studies (history, geography)	1	2	3	4	5
(f) Art	1	2	3	4	5
(g) Music	1	2	3	4	5

22. (a) How many children are there in the family?
　　　1　2　3　4　5　6　7　8　9　10
　　(b) Then ask (i)　what are their ages (listing from eldest to youngest, including X)?
　　　　　　　　(ii)　where do the children live, at home or away?
　　　　　　　　(iii)　are they male or female?
　　　　　　　　(iv)　what are their expected occupations if the children are still at school?
　　　　　　　　(v)　what is the child's present occupation if the child has left school (put university or college, if attending a tertiary institution)?

Complete the following table:

Child Number	Age of child	Residence Home Away		Sex M F		Expected occupation	Present occupation
1		1	2	1	2		
2		1	2	1	2		
3		1	2	1	2		
4		1	2	1	2		
5		1	2	1	2		
6		1	2	1	2		

7	1	2	1	2
8	1	2	1	2
9	1	2	1	2
10	1	2	1	2
11	1	2	1	2
12	1	2	1	2

23. If the child has older brothers or sisters ask: How often does X get together with any older brothers or sisters to get help with homework or reading?

very often	1
often	2
sometimes	3
not very often	4
hardly ever	5
never, or no older brothers or sisters	6

other answer (specify): _____

24. If X has younger brothers or sisters ask: How often does X get together with younger brothers or sisters and play at teaching them?

very often	1
often	2
sometimes	3
not very often	4
hardly every	5
never, or no younger brothers or sisters	6

25. (a) Did any other adults live with you before X started school (i.e. adults who stayed longer than six months)?
    1   no other adults
    2   just one
    3   2 or 3
    4   4 or 5
    5   more than 5

    (b) How often did these other adults speak English in the home?
    1   no adults, or none of them spoke English
    2   generally did not speak English
    3   half English, half another language
    4   mainly English but some other language
    5   all English
    other answer (specify): _____

(c) How much time did X spend with these other adults?
    1   no other adults, or no time
    2   not very much time
    3   quite a lot of time
    4   nearly all the time
26 (a) How many other adults live with you now?
    1   no other adults
    2   just one adult
    3   2 or 3
    4   4 or 5
    5   more than five
  (b) How often do these other adults speak English in the home?
    1   no adults, or do not speak English
    2   generally do not speak English
    3   half English, half another language
    4   mainly English but some other language
    5   all English
    other answer (specify): ──────────────────────
  (c) How much time does X spend with these other adults?
    1   no other adults, or no time
    2   not very much time
    3   quite a lot of time
    4   nearly all the time

Part B

1. How much education do you *want* X to receive?

Mother	Father	
1	1	postgraduate education (a higher degree)
2	2	graduate from university (a first degree)
3	3	at least some university
4	4	high school plus teacher training college or some other professional training college
5	5	finish high school or, as much school as possible
6	6	leave school as soon as possible

other answer: ────────────────────────────

2. How much education do you really *expect* X to receive?

Mother	Father	
1	1	postgraduate education
2	2	graduate from university
3	3	at least some university
4	4	high school plus professional training college
5	5	finish high school or, as much as possible
6	6	leave school as soon as possible

other answer: ────────────────────────────

3. How long have you had these ideas about the amount of education you expect X to receive?

Mother Father
  1   1   since X was born
  2   2   before X started school
  3   3   just after X started school
  4   4   since last year
  5   5   just this year

4. What kind of job would you really *like* X to have when she/he grows up, if at all possible?

Mother Father
  1   1   job requiring postgraduate education or long period at university (doctor, lawyer, dentist, scientist, professor,...)
  2   2   job requiring university degree (architect, public servant, engineer, high-school teacher,...)
  3   3   parents have high educational expectations (see questions 1, 2) and they state that 'it is up to the child to decide'.
  4   4   job requiring high school graduation and some college training (draughtsman, elementary–school teacher, journalist, nurse,...)
  5   5   job requiring some high school education
  6   6   job requiring little education or, parents have low educational expectations (see questions 1, 2) and they state that 'it is up to the child to decide' or, 'I don't care'.

Name of job desired: ——————————————————
other answer: —————————————————————

5. Do you really think that X *will* become a (name the job just mentioned)?

Mother Father
  1   1   Yes (emphatically)
  2   2   I hope so
  3   3   No (I don't think so), or parents indicate that it is up to the child to decide, or parents say they don't care

other answer: —————————————————————

6. How long have you had these ideas about the kind of job you would like X to have?

Mother Father
  1   1   since X was born
  2   2   before X started school
  3   3   just after X started school
  4   4   since last year
  5   5   just this year

7. What jobs do the parents have?

Mother Father
  1   1   job requiring highest education level
  2   2   job requiring university degree
  3   3   job requiring high school plus some professional col-

		lege training
4	4	job requiring some high school education
5	5	job requiring little education
6	6	no job

name the job: ─────────────

8. (a) Would the parent like to change her/his job, or is she/he happy to stay in present job?

Mother	Father	
1	1	Yes: would like to change
2	2	No: is content to stay in present job
3	3	No job

(b) If Yes, ask: Has the parent made any plans which might allow her/him to change jobs?

1	1	Yes
2	2	No

(c) If Yes, ask: what are the plans?

1	1	already attending courses (school, college ...)
2	2	taking correspondence courses
3	3	has enrolled in courses to take in future
4	4	plans to take courses in the future

other answer: ─────────────

9. How often is English spoken in the home (especially for non-English-speaking families)?

Mother	Father	Child	
1	1	1	all the time
2	2	2	over half the time (most of the time)
3	3	3	half the time
4	4	4	less than half the time
5	5	5	never or hardly ever

10. How particular would you say you are about the way X speaks English (good vocabulary, correct grammar ...)?

Mother	Father	
1	1	very strict
2	2	quite strict
3	3	not too particular
4	4	don't really care
5	5	unable to help

other answer: ─────────────

11. For non-English-speaking families:
How particular are you about the way X speaks (state the ethnic language of the family)?

Mother	Father	
1	1	very strict
2	2	quite particular
3	3	not too particular
4	4	don't really care
5	5	unable to help

12. For non-English-speaking families:
    How important is it to you that (name the ethnic language) should be
    maintained in the family and that X should speak it fluently?
    Mother   Father
    1   1   extremely important
    2   2   important
    3   3   not really important
    4   4   don't care
13. Do you have time to read books. If yes, ask how many books would you
    generally read in a month?
    (Ask for books written in English and in ethnic language.)
    Mother   Father
    1   1   no books read
    2   2   less than one a month
    3   3   about one or two a month
    4   4   3 to 5 a month (about one a week)
    5   5   6 to 10 a month (about 2 a week)
    6   6   more than 10
14. (a) When X was small, before she/he started school, did parents ever
        read to X. If yes, ask how often?
        Mother   Father
        1   1   no reading to child
        2   2   not very often, less than once a week
        3   3   about once a week
        4   4   a couple of times a week
        5   5   nearly every day (3 to 5 times a week)
        6   6   just about every day (6 or 7)
    (b) In what language did the parents generally read to X?
        Mother   Father
        1   1   English
        2   2   Italian
        3   3   Greek
        4   4   Dutch
        5   5   German
        6   6   Polish
        other language (specify): ─────────────────
15. (a) Does the mother or father ever listen to X read to them?
        If Yes: ask how often?
        Mother   Father
        1   1   just about every day (6 or 7 times)
        2   2   nearly every day (3 to 5 times a week)
        3   3   a couple of times a week
        4   4   about once a week
        5   5   less than once a week (not very often)
        6   6   never listens
    (b) In what language does X generally read to the parents?
        1   English

    2   Italian
    3   Greek
    4   Dutch
    5   German
    6   Polish
    other language (specify): ————————————

16. Does X bring home books to read, either from local library, school library, or friend's place? If yes, ask how many each month? (Ask for books written in English and in ethnic language.)
    1   no books brought home, or I don't know
    2   1 or 2 (very rarely brings books home)
    3   3 to 5 (about 1 a week)
    4   6 to 10 (about 2 a week)
    5   more than 10

17. (a) Do you think that children who are about 10 years old should be restricted from viewing certain types of TV programmes or should they decide themselves what to watch?
      1   should be restricted from certain programmes
      2   decide themselves
   (b) What about books and comics, should parents restrict 10-year-olds from reading certain types of material?
      1   Yes
      2   No
   (c) How often would you check to see what X is reading or watching on TV?
      1   never check
      2   only occasional checks
      3   quite regular checks
      4   very regular checks
      5   check most viewing and reading

18. At what age did you or would you expect X to be allowed to do the following by herself/himself?

(a) earn own spending money   6 7 8 9 10 11 12 13 14 15 16

(b) be able to undress and go to bed by herself/himself   6 7 8 9 10 11 12 13 14 15 16

(c) to know her/his way around the neighbourhood so she/he can play where she/he wants to without getting lost   6 7 8 9 10 11 12 13 14 15 16

(d) to make friends and visit their homes   6 7 8 9 10 11 12 13 14 15 16

(e) to stay alone at home at night   6 7 8 9 10 11 12 13 14 15 16

(f) to make decisions like choosing clothes or deciding how to spend money   6 7 8 9 10 11 12 13 14 15 16

(g) to act as a babysitter at someone else's home   6 7 8 9 10 11 12 13 14 15 16

(h) to sleep at a friend's home
overnight   6 7 8 9 10 11 12 13 14 15 16

(i) go to the movies alone   6 7 8 9 10 11 12 13 14 15 16

(j) go on an overnight trip organised
by the school   6 7 8 9 10 11 12 13 14 15 16

19. Do the parents ever discuss X's progress at school?
If Yes, ask how often.
1   never discuss progress
2   not very often, less than once a week
3   a couple of times a week
4   nearly every day (3 or 4 times a week)
5   every school day

20. If you see that X is having real difficulty with something she/he is doing (like building a model, fixing a toy, doing homework ...) what would you generally do?
Read alternatives:

Mother	Father	
1	1	generally, do it for X
2	2	sit down with X and help
3	3	offer to help
4	4	wait for X to ask for help, and then show X how to do it
5	5	wait for X to ask for help, but insist that X continue to do it by herself/himself

21. What educational level did the parents reach?

	Mother	Father
Higher degree level	7	7
University degree	6	6
High school plus teachers college or other college	5	5
Finished high school	4	4
Some high school	3	3
Finished primary school	2	2
Less than primary school completed	1	1

22. How many hours a day does the father, mother and child watch TV?

	Mother	Father	Child
Never watches it	1	1	1
Less than 1 hour per day	2	2	2
Between 1 and 3 hours a day	3	3	3
Between 4 and 5 hours a day	4	4	4
More than 5 hours a day	5	5	5

23. How often would you help X with her/his English grammar (e.g. tell X how to construct sentences, when to use certain words, ...)?

Mother	Father	
1	1	never
2	2	probably less than once a week
3	3	probably once a week
4	4	about a couple of times a week

5	5	probably nearly every day
6	6	every day give X some help

24. For non-English-speaking families
    How often would you help X with her/his (name the ethnic language) grammar (e.g. tell X how to construct sentences, when to use certain words,...)?

Mother   Father

1	1	never
2	2	probably less than once a week
3	3	probably once a week
4	4	about a couple of times a week
5	5	probably nearly every day
6	6	every day give X some help

25. At mealtimes who does most of the talking?
    1   everybody participates (parents and children)
    2   the parents do most of the talking
    3   father dominates the conversation
    4   mother dominates the conversation
    5   no-one is allowed to talk
    other answer: ─────────────────────────────────

26. How often do you think that children should be involved in making family decisions; such as what the family should do at weekends, where to go for holidays, what items of furniture should be bought for the home? (Ask the question in two sections: first related to 10-year-olds, and second, to 18-year-olds.)

	for 10-year-olds	for 18-year-olds
Children should never be consulted	1	1
Children should rarely be consulted	2	2
Children should be consulted on decisions which affect them	3	3
Children should be consulted on most decisions regarding the family	4	4
Children should always be included in discussions about family plans	5	5
other answer (specify): ────────────────────		

27. If children do well in their schoolwork, do you think parents should praise them?
    If yes ask: how often do you praise X for work at school?

Mother   Father

1	1	no praise given
2	2	probably less than once a week
3	3	about once a week
4	4	a couple of times a week
5	5	every day, or nearly every day

28. How much time do you think a 10- or 11-year-old should spend doing homework or schoolwork at home?

Mother	Father	
1	1	no time
2	2	about 15 minutes most days
3	3	about half an hour
4	4	nearly an hour most days
5	5	more than an hour most days

29. Do you expect X to do homework or schoolwork at home?
    If yes, ask about how much each day?

Mother	Father	
1	1	no time expected
2	2	about 15 minutes most days
3	3	about half an hour most days
4	4	nearly an hour most days
5	5	more than an hour most days

30. After the evening meal what does the family generally do?

	Mother	Father	Child
Watches TV or listens to the radio	1	1	1
Reads and watches some TV or listens to some radio	2	2	2
Mainly reads	3	3	3
Gets involved with some hobby	4	4	4
Go to bed, or go to work	5	5	5

other answer (specify):   Father ————————————————
                           Mother ————————————————
                           Child   ————————————————

31. As well as yourselves, are there any other people either inside or outside the family who regularly tell X of the importance of education? If yes, ask who. (Circle the appropriate persons, and list others.)
    1 no-one
    2 grandparent
    3 neighbour
    4 older brother
    5 older sister
    6 relative (indicate who) ——————————————————
    7 others (list them)   ——————————————————
                                ——————————————————
                                ——————————————————

32. The next question is trying to determine which parent generally makes decisions in the family.

	Mother	Father	Both parents
For example, who generally makes decisions about the purchase of X's clothes	1	2	3
What about money matters, such as whether X should be allowed to have any allowance or pocket money	1	2	3

Who would decide if X could go out

at night or go somewhere on the weekend	1	2	3
Who will decide when X should leave school	1	2	3
Who would generally make the decision whether X should spend some time doing homework or not	1	2	3
Who would generally make the decisions about what time X should go to bed	1	2	3

33. How many outside activities have the parents and X engaged in together during the past six months?
    1 a great variety of activities (some nearly every week)
    2 a moderate variety of activities (about one a week)
    3 very few activities (one or two a month)
    4 rarely go out together, or never

34. What level of education would you say that most of your close friends reached?

Mother	Father	
1	1	all or most of them graduated from university
2	2	most went onto teachers college or some other professional college after school
3	3	most completed high school
4	4	most dropped out of high school
5	5	most of them completed primary school
6	6	most of them left before the end of primary school

35. Would you know what topic X is studying (or has just finished doing) in say, English or Arithmetic, at school?

Mother	Father	
1	1	has no idea of the topics
2	2	has no idea of present topics but mentions some earlier topics that were studied
3	3	indicates uncertainty about the general topics (e.g. I think it is fractions)
4	4	knows general topic (e.g. it is fractions)
5	5	indicates uncertainty about the specific topic (e.g. I think that it is addition of fractions)
6	6	knows specific topics (e.g. division of fractions)

36. Now for the last question:
    How do you react to the following statements (agree strongly (1), agree (2), don't know (3), disagree (4), disagree strongly (5))?

	agree strongly	agree	don't know	disagree	disagree strongly
(a) Even when a boy gets married, his main loyalty still belongs to his parents	1	2	3	4	5

(b) When a girl gets married, her main loyalty still belongs to her parents   1   2   3   4   5

(c) When the time comes for a son to take a job, he should try and stay near his parents, even if it means giving up a good job opportunity   1   2   3   4   5

(d) When the times comes for a daughter to take a job, she should try and stay near her parents, even if it means giving up a good job opportunity   1   2   3   4   5

(e) Nothing in life is worth the sacrifice of moving away from one's parents   1   2   3   4   5

(f) If a family cannot afford to provide education for all their children after high school then any boys in the family should get preference   1   2   3   4   5

Appendix B*

Children's School Attitude Schedule

1. I get on well with my teachers
2. School is boring
3. I like doing hard sums in arithmetic
4. I enjoy reading
5. I like fooling about in class
6. I get a lot of my sums wrong in arithmetic
7. I think that I am pretty good at my schoolwork
8. School lessons are boring
9. When the teacher goes out of the room I play about
10. I'm sorry when school is over for the day
11. Of all the classes in this school, my class is the nicest of all
12. Generally, I have no-one to play with at lunchtime
13. In this class we spend too much time doing arithmetic
14. Sometimes I think that I am no good at anything
15. My teacher thinks that I am clever
16. If I don't understand something in class, I am too scared to ask my teacher for help
17. My teacher is always getting cross at me
18. I like other people in this class who get me into trouble
19. If I missed out on playing sports I'd be very disappointed
20. I would like to be better at sports than at school work
21. I would rather be in my class than in any other class in this school
22. I think that going out to work would be better than coming to school
23. I have no friends who I like very much in this school
24. My schoolwork worries me
25. My best friend also comes to this school
26. When the teacher asks me a question about my work I get very upset
27. When we have work to do I get very good marks
28. In this class our lessons are very interesting

*As indicated in Chapter 2, the following schedule was adapted from Barker Lunn's (1969, 1970) research on children's school-related attitudes. The responses to each statement were rated on a five-point scale, ranging from strong agreement to strong disagreement. A set of practice examples was provided and discussed with the children.

29. Children in this class who can't do their schoolwork feel ashamed
30. I don't like children who are noisy in class
31. I like children who get me into trouble
32. My teacher is interested in me
33. My class gets blamed for things we don't do
34. School is fun
35. Our teacher treats us as if we were babies
36. I think the other children in my class like me
37. I'd prefer to be in another class
38. I find a lot of schoolwork hard to understand
39. I would like to be one of the cleverest students in the school
40. I work and try very hard in school
41. I am very good at reading
42. I like most of my schoolwork
43. Going to school is a waste of time
44. I wish that there were nicer children in this class
45. My teacher is nice to me
46. I'm useless at schoolwork
47. My teacher thinks that I am a troublemaker
48. Nobody cares about us in my class
49. I like school
50. The other children in this school are very friendly
51. I would leave school tomorrow if I could
52. I hate being in this class
53. Doing well at school is most important to me
54. At school they make you do things you don't want to do
55. I enjoy it when the teacher asks me questions
56. It doesn't bother me if I get my work wrong
57. I like being in my class
58. I would like to be very good at schoolwork
59. If I don't understand something, I ask the teacher
60. My teacher likes me

Bibliography

Acland, H. (1975), 'Parents love schools', *Interchange*, 6, pp. 1–10.

Aiken, L. R. (1970), 'Attitudes towards mathematics', *Review of Educational Research*, 40, pp. 551–96.

Aiken, L. R. (1976), 'Update on attitudes and other affective variables in learning mathematics', *Review of Educational Research*, 46, pp. 293–311.

Aiken, L. R. and Dreger, R. M. (1961), 'The effect of attitudes on performance in mathematics', *Journal of Educational Psychology*, 52, pp. 19–24.

Alexander, K. L. and Eckland, B. K. (1974), 'Sex differences in the educational attainment process', *American Sociological Review*, 39, pp. 668–81.

Alexander, K. L., Eckland, B. K. and Griffin, L. J. (1975), 'The Wisconsin model of socioeconomic achievement: a replication', *American Journal of Sociology*, 81, pp. 324–42.

Alwin, D. F. and Otto, L. B. (1977), 'High school context effects on aspirations', *Sociology of Education*, 50, pp. 259–73.

Anderson, J. G. and Evans, F. B. (1976), 'Family socialization and educational achievement in two cultures: Mexican-American and Anglo-American', *Sociometry*, 39, pp. 209–22.

Argyle, M. (1976), 'Personality and social behaviour', in R. Harré (ed.), *Personality* (Oxford: Blackwell).

Armor, D. J. (1972), 'School and family effects on black and white achievement: a reexamination of the USOE data', in F. Mosteller and D. P. Moynihan (eds), *On Equality of Educational Opportunity* (New York: Random House).

Armor, D. J. (1974), 'Theta reliability and factor scaling', in H. L. Costner (ed.), *Sociological Methodology, 1973–1974* (San Francisco: Jossey Bass).

Banks, O. (1976), *The Sociology of Education* (New York: Schocken Books).

Baratz, S. S. and Baratz, J. C. (1970), 'Early childhood intervention: the social science based on institutional racism', *Harvard Educational Review*, 40, pp. 29–50.

Barker Lunn, J. C. (1969), 'The development of scales to measure junior school children's attitudes', *British Journal of Educational Psychology*, 39, pp. 64–71.

Barker Lunn, J. C. (1970), *Streaming in the Primary School* (London: NFER).

Barnes, J. (1975) (ed.), *Educational Priority. Volume 3: Curriculum Innovation in London's E.P.A.s* (London: HMSO).

Batten, E. (1975), 'Attainment, environment and education', in J. Rushton and J. D. Turner (eds), *Education and Deprivation* (Manchester: University Press).

Bell, D. (1977), 'On meritocracy and equality', in J. Karabel and A. H. Halsey (eds), *Power and Ideology in Education* (New York: Oxford University Press).

Berger, P. L. and Luckmann, T. (1971), *The Social Construction of Reality* (Harmondsworth: Penguin Books).

Bernstein, B. (1970), 'Education cannot compensate for society', *New Society*, 26, pp. 344–47.

Bernstein, B. (1977), *Class, Codes and Control. Volume 3* (London: Routledge & Kegan Paul).

Bernstein B. and Davies, B. (1969), 'Some sociological comments on Plowden', in R. Peters (ed.), *Perspectives on Plowden* (London: Routledge & Kegan Paul).

Bidwell, C. E. (1972), 'Schooling and socialization for moral commitment', *Interchange*, 3, pp. 1–27.

Bidwell, C. E. (1973), 'The social psychology of teaching', in R. M. W. Travers (ed.), *Second Handbook of Research on Teaching* (Chicago: Rand McNally).

Bloom, B. S. (1964), *Stability and Change in Human Characteristics* (New York: John Wiley).

Boudon, R. (1974), *Education, Opportunity and Social Inequality* (New York: John Wiley).

Bourdieu, P. (1973), 'Cultural reproduction and social reproduction', in R. Brown (ed.), *Knowledge, Education, and Cultural Change* (London: Tavistock).

Bradley, R. H. and Caldwell, B. M. (1976), 'The relation of infants' home environments to mental test performance at fifty-four months: a follow-up study', *Journal of Educational Psychology*, 47, pp. 1172–74.

Bradley, R. H. and Caldwell, B. M. (1977), 'Home observation for measurement of the environment: a validation study of screening efficiency', *American Journal of Mental Deficiency*, 81, pp. 417–20.

Brodie, T. A. (1964), 'Attitude toward school and academic achievement', *Personnel and Guidance Journal*, 43, pp. 375–78.

Bronfenbrenner, U. (1974), *A Report of Longitudinal Evaluations of Preschool Programs* (Washington: US Department of HEW).

Bronfenbrenner, U. (1977), 'Toward an experimental ecology of human development', *American Psychologist*, 32, pp. 513–531.

Bullock Report (1975), *A Language for Life* (London: HMSO).

Butler, N. R. and Kellmer Pringle, M. L. (1967), 'First report of the national child development study' in B. Plowden, *Children and their Primary Schools* (London: HMSO).

Bynner, J. M. (1972), *Parents' Attitudes to Education* (London: HMSO).

Bynner, J. M. (1975), 'Parents' attitudes to education and their consequences for working-class children', in J. Rushton and J. D. Turner (eds), *Education and Deprivation* (Manchester: University Press).

Coleman Report (1966), *Equality of Educational Opportunity* (Washington: Government Printing Office).

Coleman, J. S. (1968), 'The concept of equality of educational opportunity', *Harvard Educational Review*, 38, pp. 7–22.

Coleman, J. S. (1972), 'The evaluation of equality of educational opportunity', in F. Mosteller and D. P. Moynihan (eds), *On Equality of Educational Opportunity* (New York: Random House).

Coleman, J. S. (1975), 'What is meant by "an equal educational opportunity"?', *Oxford Review of Education*, 1, pp. 27–29.

Connell, R. W. (1972), 'Class structure and personal socialisation', in F. J. Hunt (ed.), *Socialisation in Australia* (Sydney: Angus & Robertson).

Connell, R. W. (1974), 'The causes of educational inequality: further observations', *Australian and New Zealand Journal of Sociology*, 10, pp. 186–89.

Cronbach, L. J. and Snow, R. E. (1977), *Aptitudes and Instructional Methods* (New York: Irvington).

Dave, R. H. (1963), 'The identification and measurement of environmental process variables that are related to educational achievement', unpublished PhD thesis (University of Chicago).

De Bord, L., Griffin, L. J. and Clark, M. (1977), 'Race, sex, and schooling: insights from the Wisconsin model of the early achievement process', *Sociology of Education*, 50, pp. 85–102.

Deutsch, M. (1967), *The Disadvantaged Child* (New York: Basic Books).

Deutsch, M. (1968), 'Field theory in social psychology', in G. Lindzey and E. Aronson (eds), *The Handbook of Social Psychology, Volume One* (Reading, Mass.: Addison-Wesley, 1968).

de Waele, J-P. and Harré, R. (1976), 'The personality of individuals', in R. Harré (ed.), *Personality* (Oxford: Blackwell).

Dyer, P. B. A. (1967), 'Home environment and achievement in Trinidad', unpublished PhD thesis (University of Alberta).

Edwards, A. D. and Hargreaves, D. H. (1976), 'The social scientific base of academic radicalism', *Educational Review*, 28, pp. 83–93.

Elardo, R., Bradley, R. H. and Caldwell, B. M. (1975), 'The relation of infants' home environments to mental test performance from six to thirty-six months: a longitudinal analysis', *Child Development*, 46, pp. 71–76.

Elardo, R., Bradley, R. H. and Caldwell, B. M. (1977), 'A longitudinal study of the relation of infants' home environments to language development at age three', *Child Development*, 48, pp. 595–603.

Endler, N. S. (1976), 'The case for person-situation interactions', in N. S. Endler and D. Magnusson (eds), *Interactional Psychology and Personality* (New York: John Wiley).

Endler, N. S. and Magnusson, D. (1976), 'Personality and person by situation interactions', in N. S. Endler and D. Magnusson (eds), *Interactional Psychology and Personality* (New York: John Wiley).

Entwistle, H. (1977), *Class, Culture and Education* (London: Methuen).

Epstein, J. L. and McPartland, J. M. (1977), 'Sex differences in family and school influence on student outcomes', Paper presented at the annual meeting of the American Sociological Association, Chicago.

Evans, F. B. and Anderson, J. G. (1973), 'The psychocultural origins of achievement and achievement motivation: the Mexican-American family', *Sociology of Education*, 46, pp. 396–416.

Eysenck, H. J. (1971), *Race, Intelligence and Education* (London: Temple Smith).

Eysenck, H. J. (1973), *Inequality of Man* (London: Temple Smith).

Featherman, D. L. and Carter, T. M. (1976), 'Discontinuities in schooling and the socioeconomic life cycle', in W. H. Sewell, R. M. Hauser and D. L.

Featherman (eds), *Schooling and Achievement in American Society* (New York: Academic Press).

Fennema, E. and Sherman, J. (1977), 'Sex-related differences in mathematics achievement, spatial visualization and affective factors', *American Educational Research Journal*, 14, pp. 51–71.

Ferguson, G. A. (1954), 'On learning and human ability', *Canadian Journal of Psychology*, 8, pp. 95–112.

Ferguson, G. A. (1956), 'On transfer of the abilities', *Canadian Journal of Psychology*, 10, pp. 121–131.

Ferri, E. (1971), *Streaming: Two Years Later* (London: NFER).

Finger, J. A. and Schlesser, G. E. (1968), 'Academic performance of public and private school students', *Journal of Educational Psychology*, 54, pp. 118–22.

Fraser, E. (1959), *Home Environment and the School* (London: University of London Press).

Freund, J. (1968), *The Sociology of Max Weber* (London: Allen Lane).

Frideres, J. (1977), 'Introduction to special issue, Ethnic Families: Structure and Interaction', *Journal of Comparative Family Studies*, 8, pp. 145–7.

Galbally Report (1978), *Migrant Services and Programs* (Canberra: Australian Government Publishing Service).

Getzels, J. W. (1969), 'A social psychology of education', in G. Lindzey and E. Aronson (eds), *The Handbook of Social Psychology, Volume Five* (Reading, Mass.: Addison-Wesley).

Giles, K. and Woolfe, R. (1977), *Deprivation, Disadvantage and Compensation* (Milton Keynes: Open University Press).

Glennerster, H. and Hatch, S. (1974) (eds), *Positive Discrimination and Inequality* (London: Fabian Society).

Goldfried, M. E. and D'Zurilla, T. J. (1973), 'Prediction of academic competence by means of the survey of study habits and attitudes', *Journal of Educational Psychology*, 64, pp. 116–22.

Good, T. L., Biddle, B. J. and Brophy, J. E. (1975), *Teachers Make a Difference* (New York: Holt, Rinehart & Winston).

Gordon, E. W. (1976), 'Group differences versus individual development in educational design', in S. Messick (ed.), *Individuality in Learning* (San Francisco: Jossey Bass).

Gordon, M. M. (1978), *Human Nature, Class, and Ethnicity* (New York: Oxford University Press).

Gramsci, A. (1971), *Prison Notebooks*, Q. Hoare and G. N. Smith (eds) (London: Lawrence and Wishart).

Guerard, A. J. (1976), *The Triumph of the Novel* (New York: Oxford University Press).

Hall, C. S. and Lindzey, G. (1970), *Theories of Personality* (New York: John Wiley).

Haller, A. O. and Portes, A. (1973), 'Status attainment processes', *Sociology of Education*, 46, pp. 51–91.

Halsey, A. H. (1972), *Educational Priority. Volume 1: E.P.A. Problems and Polices* (London: HMSO).

Halsey, A. H. (1975), 'Sociology and the equality debate', *Oxford Review of Education*, 1, pp. 9–23.

Harré, R. (1976), 'Living up to a name', in R. Harré (ed.), *Personality* (Oxford: Blackwell).

Harré, R. and Secord, P. F. (1972), *The Exploration of Social Behaviour* (Oxford: Blackwell).

Harris, A. (1974), 'Book review of Tinker, Tailor . . . The Myth of Cultural Deprivation', *The Sociological Review*, 22, p. 428.

Hauser, R. M., Sewell, W. H. and Alwin, D. F. (1976), 'High school effects on achievement', in W. H. Sewell *et al.* (eds), *Schooling and Achievement in American Society* (New York: Academic Press).

Havighurst, R. J. (1976), 'The relative importance of social class and ethnicity in human development', *Human Development*, 19, pp. 56–64.

Hearn, J. C. and Moos, R. H. (1978), 'Subject matter and classroom climate: a test of Holland's environmental propositions', *American Educational Research Journal*, 15, pp. 111–24.

Herrnstein, R. J. (1973), *I. Q. in the Meritocracy* (Boston: Atlantic Press).

Hoffman, L. (1972), 'Early childhood experiences and women's achievement motives', *Journal of Social Issues*, 28, pp. 129–55.

Hout, M. and Morgan, R. W. (1975), 'Race and sex variations in the causes of the expected attainments of high school seniors', *American Journal of Sociology*, 81, pp. 364–94.

Husén, T., Fägerlind, I. and Liljefors, R. (1974), 'Sex differences in science achievement and attitudes: a Swedish analysis by grade level', *Comparative Education Review*, 18, pp. 292–304.

Hutt, C. (1972), 'Sex differences in human development', *Human Development*, 15, pp. 153–70.

Insel, P. M. and Moos, R. H. (1974), 'Psychological environments: expanding the scope of human ecology', *American Psychologist*, 29, pp. 179–188.

Jackson, P. W. (1968), *Life in Classrooms* (New York: Holt, Rinehart & Winston).

Jackson, P. W. and Lahaderne, H. M. (1967), 'Scholastic success and attitude toward school in a population of sixth graders', *Journal of Educational Psychology*, 58, pp. 15–18.

Jencks, C. (1972), *Inequality: A Reassessment of the Effect of Family and Schooling in America* (New York: Basic Books).

Jensen, A. R. (1969), 'How much can we boost I Q and scholastic achievement?', *Harvard Educational Review*, 39, pp. 1–123.

Jensen, A. R. (1973a), *Educational Differences* (London: Methuen).

Jensen, A. R. (1973b), *Educability and Group Differences* (London: Methuen).

Johnson, D. W. (1974), 'Affective outcomes', in H. J. Walberg (ed.), *Evaluating Educational Performance* (Berkeley: McCutchan).

Kahn, S. B. (1969), 'Affective correlates of academic achievement', *Journal of Educational Psychology*, 60, pp. 216–21.

Karabel, J. and Halsey, A. H. (1977) (eds), *Power and Ideology in Education* (New York: Oxford University Press).

Keddie, N. (1972), Social differentiation II', in *School and Society* (Milton

Keynes: Open University Press).

Keddie, N. (1973), (ed.), *Tinker, Tailor ... The Myth of Cultural Deprivation* (London: Penguin Education).

Keeves, J. P. (1972), *Educational Environment and Student Achievement* (Stockholm: Almquist & Wiksell).

Keeves, J. P. (1974), 'Educational environment and student achievement', in K. Marjoribanks (ed.), *Environments for Learning (Windsor: NFER)*.

Kellaghan, T. (1977), 'Relationship between home environment and scholastic behavior in a disadvantaged population', Journal of Educational Psychology, 69, pp. 754–60.

Kerckhoff, A. C. and Campbell, R. T. (1977), 'Black-white differences in the educational attainment process', *Sociology of Education*, 50, pp. 15–27.

Kish, L. (1965), *Survey Sampling* (New York: John Wiley).

Labov, W. (1968), *A Study of the Non-Standard English of Negro and Puerto Rican Speakers in New York City, Volume Two* (New York: Columbia University).

Lambert, W. E. and Tucker, G. R. (1972), *Bilingual Education of Children* (Rowley, Mass.: Newbury House).

Lavin, D. E. (1965), *The Prediction of Academic Performance: A Theoretical Analysis and Review of Research* (New York: Russell Sage Foundation).

Lee, P. C. and Gropper, N. B. (1974), 'Sex-role culture and educational practice', *Harvard Educational Review*, 44, pp. 369–410.

Lesser, G. S. (1976), 'Cultural differences in learning and thinking styles', in S. Messick (ed.), *Individuality in Learning* (San Francisco: Jossey Bass).

Levin, H. M. (1976), 'A new model of school effectiveness', in W. H. Sewell, R. M. Hauser and D. L. Featherman (eds), *Schooling and Achievement in American Society* (New York: Academic Press).

Levine, D. U., Lachowicz, H., Oxam, K. and Tangeman, A. (1972), 'The home environment of students in a high achieving inner-city parochial school and a nearby public school', *Sociology of Education*, 45, pp. 435–45.

Lewin, K. (1935), *A Dynamic Theory of Personality* (New York: Academic Press).

Little, A. and Smith, G. (1972), *Strategies of Compensation: A Review of Educational Projects for the Disadvantaged in the United States* (London: OECD).

Longstreth, L. E. (1978), 'A comment on "Race, IQ, and the Middle Class" by Trotman: rampant false conclusions', *Journal of Educational Psychology*, 70, pp. 469–72.

Lueptow, L. B. (1975), 'Parental status and influence and the achievement orientations of high school seniors', *Sociology of Education*, 48, pp. 91–110.

Maccoby, E. E. (1966), *The Development of Sex Differences* (London: Tavistock).

Maccoby, E. E. and Jacklin, C. N. (1974), *The Psychology of Sex Differences* (Stanford: Stanford University Press).

Malpass, L. F. (1953), 'Some relationships between students' perceptions of school and their achievement', *Journal of Educational Psychology*, 44, pp. 475–82.

Marjoribanks, K. (1972*a*), 'Environment, social class, and mental abilities', *Journal of Educational Psychology*, 63, pp. 103–9.

Marjoribanks, K. (1972*b*), 'Ethnic and environmental influences on mental abilities', *American Journal of Sociology*, 78, pp. 323–37.

Marjoribanks, K. (1974*a*), *Environments for Learning* (Windsor: NFER).

Marjoribanks, K. (1974*b*), 'Another view of the relation of environment to mental abilities', *Journal of Educational Psychology*, 66, pp. 460–3.

Marjoribanks, K. (1976*a*), 'Sibsize, family environment, cognitive performance, and affective characteristics', *Journal of Psychology*, 94, pp. 195–204.

Marjoribanks, K. (1976*b*), 'Social learning theory and the family: an analysis', *Psychology in the Schools*, 13, pp. 457–62.

Marjoribanks, K. (1976*c*), 'School attitudes, cognitive ability, and academic achievement', *Journal of Educational Psychology*, 68, pp. 653–60.

Marjoribanks, K. (1977*a*), 'Affective and environmental correlates of cognitive performance', *Journal of Educational Research*, 70, pp. 3–8.

Marjoribanks, K. (1977*b*), 'Socioeconomic status and its relation to cognitive performance as mediated through the family environment', in A. Oliverio (ed.), *Genetics, Environment and Intelligence* (Amsterdam: Biomedical Press).

Marjoribanks, K. (1978*a*), 'Family and school environmental correlates of school-related affective characteristics: An Australian Study', *Journal of Social Psychology*, 106, pp. 181–89.

Marjoribanks, K. (1978*b*), 'Personality and environmental correlates of cognitive performance and school related affective characteristics: a regression surface analysis', *Alberta Journal of Educational Research*, 24, pp. 230–243.

Marjoribanks, K. (1978*c*), 'Ethnicity, school attitudes, intelligence and academic achievement', *International Journal of Psychology*, 13, pp. 167–78.

Marjoribanks, K. (1978*d*), 'Ethnicity, family environment, school attitudes and academic achievement, *Australian Journal of Education*, 22, pp. 249–61.

Marjoribanks, K. (1979*a*), *Families and their Learning Environments* (London: Routledge & Kegan Paul).

Marjoribanks, K. (1979*b*), 'Family environments', in H. J. Walberg (ed.), *Educational Environments and Effects: Evaluation, Research and Policy* (Berkeley: McCutchan).

Marjoribanks, K. (1979*c*), 'Family and school environmental correlates of intelligence, personality, and school-related affective characteristics', *Genetic Psychology Monographs*, 99, pp. 165–83.

Marjoribanks, K. (1979*d*), 'Ethnicity, family environment and cognitive performance: a regression surface analysis'. *Journal of Comparative Family Studies* 10, pp. 5–18.

Marsh, P., Rosser, E. and Harré, R. (1978), *The Rules of Disorder* (London: Routledge & Kegan Paul).

McBee, G. and Duke, R. L. (1960), 'Relationship between intelligence, scholastic motivation, and academic achievement', *Psychological Reports*, 3, pp. 3–8.

Merton, R. K. (1968), *Social Theory and Social Structure* (New York: The Free Press).

Merton, R. K. (1976), *Sociological Ambivalence and Other Essays* (New York: The Free Press).

Midwinter, E. (1975), 'Towards a solution of the EPA problem: the community school', in J. Rushton and J. D. Turner (eds), *Education and Deprivation* (Manchester: University Press).

Midwinter, E. (1977), *Education for Sale* (London: George Allen & Unwin).

Moore, T. (1967), 'Language and intelligence: a longitudinal study of the first eight years. Part i. Patterns of development in boys and girls, *Human Development*, 10, pp. 88–106.

Moore, T. (1968), 'Language and intelligence: a longitudinal study of the first eight years. Part ii. Environmental correlates of mental growth, *Human Development*, 11, pp. 1–24.

Moos, R. H. (1973), 'Conceptualizations of human environments', *American Psychologist*, 28, pp. 652–65.

Moos, R. H. (1974), *Evaluating Treatment Environments* (New York: John Wiley).

Moos, R. H. (1975), *Evaluating Correctional and Community Settings* (New York: John Wiley).

Moos, R. H. (1978), 'A typology of junior high and high school classrooms', *American Educational Research Journal*, 15, pp. 53–66.

Moos, R. H. (1979), *Evaluating Educational Environments* (San Francisco: Jossey Bass).

Moos, R. H. and Moos, B. S. (1976), 'A typology of family social environments', *Family Process*, 15, pp. 357–371.

Morrison, C. M. (1974), (ed.), *Educational Priority. Volume 5: E.P.A.-A Scottish Study* (Edinburgh: HMSO).

Mosteller, F. and Moynihan, D. P. (1972) (eds), *On Equality of Educational Opportunity* (New York: Random House).

Mosychuk, H. (1969), 'Differential home environments and mental ability patterns', unpublished PhD thesis (University of Alberta).

Murray, H. (1938), *Explorations in Personality* (Oxford: University Press).

Newbold, D. (1977), *Ability Grouping: the Banbury Enquiry* (Windsor: NFER).

Parsons, T. (1951), *The Social System* (London: Routledge & Kegan Paul).

Peaker, G. F. (1967), 'The regression analysis of the national survey', in B. Plowden, *Children and their Primary Schools, Volume Two* (London: HMSO).

Peaker, G. F. (1971), *The Plowden Children Four Years Later* (Windsor: NFER).

Persell, C. H. (1977), *Education and Inequality: A Theoretical and Empirical Synthesis* (New York: Free Press).

Picou, J. S. and Carter, T. M. (1976), 'Significant-other influence and aspirations', *Sociology of Education*, 49, pp. 12–22.

Pilling, D. and Kellmer Pringle, M. L. (1978), *Controversial Issues in Child Development* (London: Paul Elek).

Plowden Report (1967), *Children and their Primary Schools* (London: HMSO).

Porter, J. (1975), 'Ethnic pluralism in Canadian perspective', in N. Glazer and D. P. Moynihan (eds), *Ethnicity* (Cambridge, Mass.: Harvard University Press).

Portes, J. N. (1976), 'Socialization and mobility in educational and early occupational attainment', *Sociology of Education*, 49, pp. 23–33.

Portes, A. and Wilson, K. L. (1976), 'Black-white differences in educational attainment', *American Sociological Review*, 41, pp. 414–31.

Presthus, R. (1962), *The Organizational Society* (New York: Random House).

Rawls, J. (1971), *A Theory of Justice* (Cambridge, Mass.: Harvard University Press).

Riessman, F. (1974), 'The hidden IQ' in A. Garter, C. Greer and F. Riessman (eds), *The New Assault of Equality: IQ and Social Stratification* (New York: Harper & Row).

Robinson, P. (1976), *Education and Poverty* (London: Methuen).

Rosen, B. C. (1956), 'The achievement syndrome: a psychocultural dimension of stratification', *American Sociological Review* , 21, pp. 203–11.

Rosen, B. C. (1959), 'Race, ethnicity, and achievement syndrome', *American Sociological Review*, 24, pp. 47–60.

Rosen, B. C. (1961), 'Family structure and achievement motivation', *American Sociological Review*, 26, pp. 574–84.

Ross, K. N. (1976), *Searching for Uncertainty* (Melbourne: Australian Council for Educational Research).

Schwartz, A. J. (1971), 'A comparative study of values and achievement: Mexican-American and Anglo Youth', *Sociology of Education*, 44. pp. 438–62.

Sewell, W. H. and Hauser, R. M. (1972), 'Causes and consequences of higher education: models of the status attainment process', *American Journal of Agricultural Economics*, 54, pp. 851–61.

Sewell, W. H. and Hauser, R. M. (1975), *Education, Occupation,and Earnings* (New York: Academic Press).

Sewell, W. H. and Hauser, R. M. (1976), 'Causes and consequences of higher education: models of the status attainment process', in W. H. Sewell *et al.* (eds), *Schooling and Achievement in American Society* (New York: Academic Press).

Shils, E. A. and Finch, H. A. (1949) (eds), *Max Weber on the Methodology of the Social Sciences* (Glencoe, Ill.: Free Press).

Shockley, W. (1971*a*), 'Negro IQ deficit: failure of a "malicious coincidence" model warrants new research proposals', *Review of Educational Research*, 41, pp. 227–48.

Shockley, W. (1971*b*), 'Models, mathematics, and the moral obligation to diagnose the origin of Negro IQ deficits', *Review of Educational Research*, 41, pp. 369–77.

Smith, G. (1975) (ed.), *Educational Priority. Volume 4: The West Riding*

Project (London: HMSO).
Smith, M. S. (1972), 'Equality of Educational Opportunity: The Basic Findings Reconsidered' in F. Mosteller and D. P. Moynihan (eds), *On Equality of Educational Opportunity* (New York: Random House).
Spencer, W. A. (1976), 'Interpersonal influences on educational aspirations: a cross-cultural analysis', *Sociology of Education*, 49, pp. 41–46.
Strodtbeck, F. L. (1958), 'Family interaction, values and achievement', in D. McClelland (ed.), *Talent and Society (Princeton, N. J. : Van Nostrand)*.
Thomas, W. I. *(1966), Social Organization and Social Personality, Selected Papers* (Chicago: University of Chicago Press).
Thomas, W. I. and Znaniecki, F. (1958), *The Polish Peasant in Europe and America* (New York: Dover Publications).
Trickett, E. J. and Moos, R. H. (1973), 'Social environment of junior high and high school classrooms', *Journal of Educational Psychology*, 64, pp. 93–102.
Trotman, F. K. (1977), 'Race, IQ, and the middle class', *Journal of Educational Psychology*, 69, pp. 266–73.
Trotman, F. K. (1978), 'Race, IQ, and rampant misinterpretations: a reply', *Journal of Educational Psychology*, 70, pp. 478–81.
Walberg, H. J. and Marjoribanks, K. (1976), 'Family environment and cognitive development: twelve analytic models', *Review of Educational Research*, 46, pp. 527–51.
Watt, J. S. (1974), 'Action in the Primary School', in C. M. Morrison (ed.), *Educational Priority. Volume 5* (London: HMSO).
Weber, M. (1948) *From Max Weber: Essays in Sociology*, H. H. Gerth and C. Wright Mills (eds) (London: Routledge & Kegan Paul).
Weiss, J. (1969), 'The identification and measurement of home environmental factors related to achievement motivation and self esteem, unpublished PhD thesis (University of Chicago).
Weiss, J. (1974), 'The identification and measurement of home environmental factors related to achievement motivation and self esteem, in K. Marjoribanks (ed.), *Environments for Learning* (Windsor: NFER).
Williams, R. L. (1970), 'Personality, ability, and achievement correlates of scholastic attitudes', *Journal of Educational Research*, 63, pp. 401–3.
Williams, T. (1976), 'Abilities and environments', in W. H. Sewell, R. M. Hauser and D. L. Featherman (eds), *Schooling and Achievement in American Society* (New York: Academic Press).
Wilson, K. L. and Portes, A. (1975), 'The educational attainment process: results from a national survey', *American Journal of Sociology*, 81, pp. 343–62.
Wiseman, S. (1967), 'The Manchester survey', in B. Plowden. *Children and their Primary Schools, Volume Two* (London: HMSO).
Wolf, R. M. (1964), 'The identification and measurement of environmental process variables related to intelligence', unpublished PhD thesis (University of Chicago).
Wolff, J. L. (1978), 'Utility of socioeconomic status as a control in racial comparisons of IQ', *Journal of Educational Psychology*, 70, pp. 473–77.

Author Index

Subject Index